250 YEARS
and STILL
A SLAVE

250 Years and Still a Slave

ISBN: 978-0-9857423-9-3

Ordering information: Quantity Sales. Special discounts are available on quantity purchases by corporations, associations, and others. For details, contact Special Sales Department at Visionary Insight Press.

Visionary Insight Press, 822 Westchester Place, Charleston, IL 61920

Visionary Insight Press, the Visionary Insight Press logo and its individual parts are trademarks of Visionary Insight Press.

Literary Executive Director: Lisa Hardwick-Peplow

250 YEARS and STILL A SLAVE

Breaking Free
with Active Centralized Empowerment:
A New Way of Thinking
and Performing

"Peace cannot be Kept by Force; it can only be achieved by understanding,"

—*Albert Einstein*

"If your success is defined as being well-adjusted to injustice and well-adapted to indifference, then we don't want successful leaders. We want great leaders-who love the people enough and respect the people enough to be unsought, unbound, unafraid, and unintimidated to tell the truth."

—*Dr. Cornel West*

"Wake Up and Live your best day, TODAY!"

—*Janice Marie Collins, Ph.D.*

Abstract

African Americans have asked for a formal apology and reparations. They have asked to be treated fairly and in a just way. They have asked for others to judge them by the content of their character and not by the color of their skin. Not because they don't like their color, rather, it is because others don't. Because of the many decades of being victims of constant racism and discriminatory acts, African Americans have developed what I call Internalized Colonization and Racial Fatigue. The symptoms and fallout from such a long period of being enslaved and being treated "less than" has been catastrophic for African Americans' engagement as a viable and productive group. As a result, in some instances, they have performed along the lines of a Self-fulfilling prophecy. However, the Self in which I am referring is one that has been prescribed by a System that operates in Hegemonic ways. Additionally, as a result, African Americans (AAs) have begun to engage in destructive and counterproductive activities that cripple group prosperity and threaten the existence of others. Unlike other aggregates, I assert that AAs do not possess a strong cultural, ethnic, or racial connection to an identity *outside* of American slavery or outside the borders of America in general. From an existentialist perspective, this form of micro-aggression through omission has caused AAs to be conditioned to perform, think, and be viewed (by him/herself and others) as slaves well after the Emancipation Proclamation. Slaves that are sociologically placed to uphold systems that can be harmful to their pursuit of life, liberty and pursuit of happiness. Until AAs change their cognitive, critical way of thinking, as well as their performance, they will remain enslaved and marginalized.

After years of study and research I have developed a theory and a practice called Active Centralized Empowerment (A.C.E.) that provides arguments as to how the System, in which we are operating in today, does not work for the African American who truly wants to be free. This System that was at one time, deliberate, is now entrenched within the walls of our being - designed to maintain the slave mentality and belief system.[1] Control the mind and design the belief system with unchallenged autonomy, one can control the person. The present System is not designed for the happiness and prosperity of the African American, therefore, there must be engagement in a *new* System. Active Centralized Empowerment (A.C.E.) is a groundbreaking, game-changing paradigm and module that has the potential to change all of Black America (this paradigm may also be used for anyone of any race, gender, sex, or ethnicity, etc., who feels marginalized). It will change how we view ourselves, consequently, how Others view and interact with us as well. This paradigm is different because it dictates *movement* to the core of power by the individuals and aggregates found in the margins.

A.C.E.'s design is holistic in nature, using analyses of research data of mixed methodologies with a central focus that covers themes of physical, structural, and social-psychological processes of anti-black violence and attitudes. My arguments take into consideration Critical Race Theory, the Framing Theory, Hegemony, Cooley's Looking Glass Self, Situated Knowledge, location and construct of Self, and the demographics of Message Designers. Ironically, I further assert that A.C.E. allows for deep introspection for Black Americans who have internalized the Oppressive message, indirectly or directly, subconsciously or consciously. It also allows for *"racist"* liberation for Black Americans as well as White Americans, by offering a *new* way to address and understand *"White Guilt, White Privilege* and *Entitlement,"* that is transformational.

A division of my studies seeks to address

possible solutions to the condition of being Black in America, African American in America and its navigation within the White Construct - a navigation that, in many instances, has placed African Americans in a psychologically inferior place of empowerment/disempowerment that is maintained and guided by Systems of Oppression, Racism and Fear. It is new and developing, but the residual effects are endless. Through the prism of A.C.E., we can move toward creating an ideal world of mutual respect and love of one another as well as compassion and empathy. A place of peace and self-empowerment.

TABLE OF CONTENTS

Abstract

***Disclaimer: Before reading further, I ask that you open your mind to the possibilities and have the courage to read the entire piece - then reflect on what I have proposed. If not, you (Black, White, or Other) will find yourself on the defensive from the beginning and absorb nothing. It is important that you place yourself in a position that will allow you to engage in, consider and ponder this new paradigm as you seek to understand this new way of existing and living. Enjoy the journey.

CHAPTER 1
RACISM: The Truth, The Problem, The Solution

After years of study and research, common themes that emerged from epistemological and ontological perspectives have illuminated the systemic problem and solution for African Americans, Black Americans. I use both descriptors because, depending on the situation, it is the Blackness that is the focus, while in others, the African. "Black" Americans represents the racial construct we became. "African" Americans represents who we are. Unlike immigrants, slaves in America, African Americans were stripped of their heritage, culture, language, history, family lineage, ancestral common grounds, ancestral pride, and ancestral roots that tied them to the global world. Before they learned to wear jeans inappropriately, became ashamed of their beautiful, naturally, curly, kinky hair that shielded them from the torcher of the essential sun[2], ashamed of their beautiful skin color that others die to have[3], ashamed of their full lips, full nose, broad hips that gave birth to all humanity ... before they were taught to be ashamed and afraid to speak up and out except when their lives were threatened, Africans who became African American slaves, had an existence of "knowing" that included freedom, Kings and Queens, chiefs and chieftesses, warriors, educators, scientists, mathematicians, philosophers and leaders ... not just of Africa, but leaders of the world. Upon arriving in America, these Africans were converted into the *political* construct of Black.

Because of how Blackness is defined and confined in this country, it has been hard for the majority of African Americans to smoothly navigate through their lives without serious challenges. It has also been challenging for them to be viewed, judged and treated fairly and objectively. I argue that one of the main reasons this occurs is because African Americans have been trying to work, live, thrive and survive within a System that was not designed or built for them, their happiness, or their prosperity. This also includes socio-economic and political aspects as well. The structure and infrastructure that embodies their lives was built to maintain the status

3

quo (mostly white, male and heterosexual in power) and to keep the marginalized under control. This was the original plan. This is not to say that there hasn't been change for the good. But, the racist System, itself, that was built hundreds and hundreds of years ago, is still operational. It has been modified and revisited, but the basic foundation has stayed much the same. Since slavery, African Americans have had to either wait for changes in others that translated into changes in policies or they have had to invent ways to circumvent certain areas of the structural design so that they can at least feel that they are living the American dream ... or knows what it looks like. Because of their Blackness, it has not been easy.

Even after the signing of the Emancipation Proclamation, many of them are still slaves mentally, psychologically and emotionally. Slaves within their own captivity because their MINDS are still enslaved. Because African Americans have consistently operated from positions of marginalization and oppression, they have been intentionally and unintentionally cultivated, conditioned, and socialized to remain oppressed. Because this acculturation made its home within the subconscious, unknowingly to its members, this group has been taught to operate and think of themselves as victims who must fight for their existence. Yes, from one perspective, the fight for one's existence is absolutely real … but perhaps the fighting involves the wrong people and the wrong things and most importantly, fighting from the wrong position and social location. Fighting only from the margins redesigns the cognitive process of an individual. This way of *thinking* AND *being* has affected African Americans negatively, both mentally and spiritually, to the depths of their psyche. It is a CONDITION. It is the Internalized Colonization of the mind, body and spirit. Simply stated, in many cases, African Americans (like many others) are not allowed to be truly free in this country.

Because this "country" known as America was organized and built <u>on the foundation of slavery</u>, the discussions around power structures are usually focused on black and white issues, literally. When we speak of racism, it is also primarily a Black and White issue because, in this country, White Americans are of the "dominant" "race," therefore, they dictate the movement and beliefs of others. They are the role models, if you will, of how Black Americans should be viewed and treated. However, I submit to you, that after 250 years, the key to solving some of the problems with African Americans does not reside solely with White people, White racists, or even a White System or institution. African American's self-empowerment will not be found or designed or even introduced to you by White America. This is not their responsibility or job or role, especially since the goal is to move *past* slavery and colonization, which means taking control of your own destiny. Certain changes will occur when the law moves in a progressive direction or when people change themselves. For now, the key to your success, your personal, emotional success lies within you, knowing who you are as a Black American, an African American, an African and an American. Second, it is also found in knowing the System in which you were placed that was not created for your empowerment must be replaced with a subsequent System that you must now create for yourself. In order to gain your empowerment, your self-empowerment, YOU must CHANGE the way you think and view your Self, your social location and MOVE to a space that is central to self-empowerment and acceptance. Active Centralized Empowerment (A.C.E.) does this. It is my position that A.C.E. can provide a basic and fundamental foundation to understanding all of the other debates, calls for action and movement in present day conversations and discourses on race.

The introduction of this paradigm, A.C.E., is holistic in nature through data gathered from research data of mixed methodologies with a central focus that covers themes of emotional, social-psychological, physical, and structural processes. My arguments take into consideration various theories, Critical

Race Theory, the Framing Theory, Hegemony, Cooley's Looking Glass Self, Situated Knowledge and location and construct of Self, and the demographics of Message Designers. This paradigm is groundbreaking in the fact that it outlines and offers solutions to the condition of being Black in America and successfully navigating within the White Systemic Construct here in this country as well as abroad, while preserving self esteem, pride, and confidence. This point is extremely important because it is my position that the minds of African Americans have been conditioned to think, therefore, perform from a disadvantaged psychological position that directly affects their ability to move through social and economic oppressions; oppressive measures that tear down the African American aggregate while benefitting the welfare of others. It is my position that in many situations, to navigate from the margins is similar to being on your back and attempting to fight upwards, never on equal footing.[4]

The Black Experience is indigenous to African Americans and until this specialized voice is heard, respected and responded to, subjects within this aggregate will continue to be vilified, nullified, even killed, senselessly. Article after article, study after study, news story after news story, and conversations after conversations reveal the lack of understanding and accepting the peculiar and particular position of Black navigation in America. This ignorance has placed Black people and, specifically, the Black male in a psychologically inferior place of empowerment that is maintained and guided by Systems of Oppression, Racism and Fear.

Quietly, slowly, methodically, this System is destroying the Black Family from the top down, as well as the potential for the African American culture to survive and flourish as a formidable, viable, essential aggregate and contributor to the Global village. If you want to understand the breakdown of the Black family all you have to do is go back hundreds of years when families were pulled apart during slavery. If you want to understand the breakdown of the Black economy simply look to the fact that African Americans were never given equal and fair footing to stand on, consistently, from the beginning and thereafter on an economic level … and they've been struggling, as a people, ever since.

With all that being said, I think it is important for the reader to understand that the institution of slavery in America has also affected White Americans and others. They, too, have been conditioned and socialized to hold certain beliefs. The belief system of constructed White American states that they must be the heroes and save other aggregates, lead other aggregates, be comfortable in a dominant, even domineering role in relation to other aggregates, and must be the ones to validate, justify, and legitimize the emotions, concerns and issues of others. In many cases, they have also been conditioned to perceive, view and interact with Black Americans, specifically, in a particular way. Through this interaction, they inherit, build and carry White privilege, White entitlement as well as White guilt. In many instances, these elements can be intentional or unintentional, subconscious or conscious. For example, some White Americans who uphold a racist and oppressive System may view African

Americans as less than or social deviants who have to be parented. This may not be how they feel, personally, but more so, how they have been dictated and conditioned to feel within a racist System. Another example of this type of manifestation is while the Black American is still in a position of some form of slavery, so is the White American who continues to be placed in positions of being perceived as a racist, a slave owner, land owner, even participating in Black image and American image ownership. Just because a person is born White does not mean that they are automatically racist. I argue that the situation at hand is that, in most cases for White Americans, from the time they are born in this country, everything that they see, hear and read primarily glorifies the White American Male and White American … with a hint of other races, colors and ethnicities here and there. Within these walls, lie constructed benefits that are oppressive to non-whites (and at times, women) and beneficial to White Americans. Just like Black Americans, White Americans and others are born into a racist infrastructure where "Whiteness" plays an integral role in sustaining a particular status quo, even without deliberate participation[5]. That is the problem. It is a particular way of living, thinking and again performing. Because the White "founding fathers" of this country designed a System that benefits a specific race, inherently so, White Americans have inherited some of the privileges of being within a White construct. But, as I just stated, they have also inherited some of its ailments and burdens. Because of this fact, in some cases, and in peculiar ways, White Americans can be victims of this oppressive, colonized, marginalized way of being and performing, as well. So, it's not entirely their fault that they develop certain beliefs. This is important to understand and embrace because, outside of intentional and direct efforts to change, humans can only do what they have been conditioned to do in most cases. Not all injustices occur because people are bad people or they have bad intentions. Rather, it is the racist infrastructure in which ALL Americans are born into that is problematic. However, I strongly believe that White Americans must engage in an introspection of their behavior, attitude and beliefs that may *sustain* a racist and discriminatory System, especially as they pertain to untruths and injustices ... or not, because freedom means having choices. In no way am I saying that individuals should not be held accountable or culpable for racist acts and deeds. What I am saying to African Americans is that you can't wait on others to change before you move towards gaining and receiving your freedom. By doing so, by waiting on the approval and validation from others, would be just another form of slavery that we are participating in.

It is time to begin your Self-Empowerment Development and Movement, the beginning of living your life as a free American, a free Black American, African American and not a slave. A.C.E. is a form of emancipation that is self-powered and empowering for the African American. Ironically, I propose that A.C.E. also allows racist liberation (incognizant or cognizant) for White Americans and Black Americans who have internalized the Oppressive message, unknowingly. My argument outlines how the American structure works on a metacognitive level consisting of three major elements that exacerbates the

Black condition followed by the solution, Active Centralized Empowerment. It is an argument that includes analyses of the grounded theories of Cooley's Looking Glass Self, Symbolic Interactionism and begins with the issue and problem of Marginalization.

CHAPTER 2
Accepted Marginalization= Accepted Oppression

Bell hooks writes, "to be in the margin is to be part of the whole but outside the main body. We could enter the world but we could not live there. We had to always return to the margin, to cross the tracks to shacks and abandoned houses on the edge of town (hooks, xvi, 1984)." She goes on to say that her families' survival as well as other blacks in her neighborhood "depended on an ongoing public awareness of the separation between margin and center and an ongoing private acknowledgement that we were a necessary, vital part of the whole." So, the outliers or outsiders or others (as they are usually labeled by the majority group) can enter a space, be a part of a space, only to uphold the power structure but never truly live within the structure in which all processes revolve. The marginalized or outside groups define and perceive themselves only in relation to the core, which means the problems and solutions are only found in the core. Simultaneously, the core, defines itself by their relation to the margins. This is the traditional, American module.

As an example, Diagram 1 illustrates how the White Heterosexual Male (WHM) constructed sense of Being and of Self is located within the Marginalization of African American males (AAM), Women (W), and individuals of the Gay and Lesbian (G/L) culture. The WHM defines himself and his role by what <u>he is not</u>. By giving meaning to what it is to be Black, to be a woman with feminine ways, and to be homosexual, dictates the image, performance and meaning of what it is to be the opposite, a White heterosexual male. This central position carries a large amount of power. To possess the power to not only define oneself as a WHM <u>in addition</u> to possessing the power to then, in turn, define who the marginalized groups are in relation to the WHM, establishes considerable power over the entire domain.

Diagram 1. Marginalization Illustrated

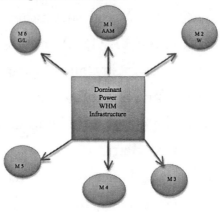

As you can see from this example and illustration, the marginalized are not allowed to move freely for their own self-preservation, self-empowerment or self-definition. They define themselves in relation to the core. If the White, heterosexual male is an actual accepted, codified, construct with power (because some researchers would argue that race itself does not exist) and this construct is embedded and protected by a racist, sexist, homophobic infrastructure of existence, it is easy to comprehend the possible and realistic oppressive power structures that exists both systemically as well as individually within this paradigm (Diagram 1[6]).

bell hooks speaks about the margin as the space she chose to work in and from. It is a political space. She is choosing the margin as a space of radical openness, possibly assisted by Harding's Standpoint Theory. Hooks argues that there is a distinctive difference between the marginality one chooses as a site of resistance and marginality that is imposed by oppressive structures. The marginal space is not a site of domination but of resistance according to hooks and "we come to this space through suffering and pain, through struggle" (Collins, p. 159, 2000). I agree with hook's stance, however, when it comes to African American males and other marginalized aggregates, I would encourage using the space of suffering pain and struggle, to initiate movement to a place of dominance. It is my position that by accepting the place of marginality, by fighting from this location, consistently, one is always on the defensive, not the offensive, which is where I believe African American arguments can be effectively engaged. Not offensive in an instigated violent way but by simply having a voice that has value and should be heard by individuals, organizations, and institutions located away from the margins. But, this is usually not the procedure.

One of the obvious examples of the toxic effect oppressive Marginalization can have on the Black community is the exploitation of Black males. Black males are kept on the margins without power through: constructive processes of image control in all forms of media, laws and policy, definitions of masculinity by the oppressors, lack of positions of real power, definitions by the Oppressor of what it is to be Black in America and Black Males in America, a continued redesigning and re-telling of a history that is inaccurate, and an absence of multi-level cultural and racial roots that allows the perpetuation of falsehoods that are subsequently used to exploit the Black male. In other words, Black Males are not allowed, encouraged, or rewarded to perform with a masculinity that exists outside of slave performance or threatens the White male power structure. They are kept on the margins without power over other masculinities because to have power *itself* is a form of masculinity. To possess this power also means that you are no longer a slave and can move freely. Freedom: freedom to be your best Self, your authentic Self, and your true Self is a luxury and privilege that many Black males have never experienced in a positive way.

Out of desperation, I propose that some Black males have found a form of "masculine" power. Unfortunately, this power is misogynistic in nature and has been used in negative ways. This is mostly represented in the entertainment industry, including music videos. There is also the continued gang violence and the glorification of violence in general. This violence is a form of "bullying" and, I propose, one of the main reasons this form of bullying occurs within the Black masculine construct is because they, themselves, Black Males, have been victims of bullying for generations, systemically and individually. Therefore, as a "natural" progression or "conversion," they have now become the bullies. The second reason for this occurrence relates to idea that the only power African American men, in general, are allowed to engage and thrive in, even receiving monetary rewards - comes through the exploitation and misogynistic attacks on women, primarily Black women. Operating from the margins creates limits. So, while the Black Male experiences forms of obstructive power, their choices of how they use this power is neither proper nor appropriate. But, perhaps, they don't feel as if they have a choice.

Another example of Marginalization along these lines is, if a White male is constructed to be the image of a Hero, the African American Male will always be the victim or adversary. Within this paradigm, the AAM must remain the victim/adversary to give the White Male a valid position as

Hero. Since the White Male is in a position of power, this process will only change if the White Male redefines his role in relation to the AAM. The AAM cannot redefine the White Male's role because their marginalized position does not grant movement within this particular power structure. The answer and solution for the AAM then is to detach from the oppressive module and operate within another module that places the marginalized individual in a position of self-empowerment. This is the basic theme of Active Centralized Empowerment; a theme I will discuss further in this paper.

To date, Marginalization exists, prevalently, in the academic world where intellectual competence is paramount and ubiquitous in its influence on American lives *outside* of the academy. The academic world mirrors the "real" world. For example, when African Americans or African American scholars speak of their hurt and pain, unless it involves guns, drugs, HIV-AIDS, or pregnancy, their voices appear to be kept outside of the hearing-range of the core. Rather, their voices are found in the margins of libraries and journals and media outlets that are connected only to the African American audiences. I assert that this is a form of micro-aggression. Because the American voices from African Americans about an American problem are kept in the margins and alcoves of what some would label "mainstream", diversity is simply a <u>theory</u> rather than a <u>practice</u> for most White Americans. On the other hand, if a *non-Black*, American, tells these same "Black" stories, then, the literature is usually found in the "mainstream" because there is an active belief that only White Americans can speak to White Americans and only White Americans will listen to White Americans (i.e. Tim Wise). While there is some truth to this assessment, I do not believe that this is the absolute truth. I believe that White Americans can and will listen to the stories of African Americans, from African Americans if their literature is moved to the "mainstream," challenging Marginalization. Yet, outside of a few choice Black authors, this form of discrimination continues. I also assert that by not challenging the Marginalization process directs an unfair judgment and misconception onto the White American and limits their knowledge base of understanding diversity. By limiting awareness and value of the marginalized is one way the power structure of the core is maintained. Therefore, to reach equality, the distribution of power must be shared.

If there is Power in the Margins like hooks and many other esteemed scholars assert, then shouldn't the knowledge attained from intersectionality (Collins), and Cross Cultural Competence found in the margins allow, empower, and encourage movement to the center, the core? Examining how the processes and theories of Cooley's *Looking Glass Self* and *Symbolic Interactionism* work in conjunction with Marginalization assists in answering this question and further supports my argument as to why these processes, that have been used for decades, is so problematic for the African American male and African Americans, in general.

CHAPTER 3
Broken Mirror and Distorted Symbolism

Everyone can be marginalized to a certain degree using Cooley's Looking Glass Self model where you define yourself by how you imagine others see you (Cooley, Mead). It is the corner stone of the Sociological Theory of Socialization. There are three main components of the *Looking Glass Self* (Yeung, Martin. 2003).

1. We imagine how we must appear to others.

2. We imagine the judgment of that appearance.

3. We develop our Self through the judgments of others.

In other words, how we see ourselves does not come from who we really are to ourselves, but rather, from how we believe others see us (Diagram 2). So, a male's parents may see him as an angel. A girlfriend may view him as a hero. A brother may view him as muscular and an ex-girlfriend may see him as a devil.

Diagram 2. Cooley's Looking Glass Self Illustrated

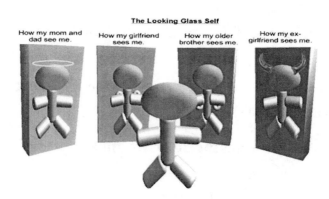

The Looking Glass Self

How my mom and dad see me.　How my girlfriend sees me.　How my older brother sees me.　How my ex-girlfriend sees me.

I challenge the use of Cooley's *Looking Glass Self* as a conduit to developing a healthy form of Self Empowerment because of the diminishing power that is so innate in the process of the individual to define oneself. My argument is, because Cooley's *Looking Glass Self* places the reference groups (peers, colleagues, significant others) outside of the individual in such a powerful role, the power of the individual person who is being judged is negated. I further argue that this module is counterproductive because it can lead to an unhealthy form of codependency. How can one build self-esteem that is sustainable if there is a constant concern about how others see us and judge us? The individual's behavior is dictated by the approval or disapproval of the reference group. Therefore, it is my contention that within this paradigm, the subject is actually being marginalized, consistently. The resulting SELF of this process moves us further away from who we really are. I propose that movement from the margins and even away from the *Looking Glass Self* allows EMPOWERMENT and LIBERATION. However, this way of thinking and performing can be extremely difficult because of Symbolic Interactionism.

Symbolic Interactionism is the way humans understand each other through constructed and accepted symbols and it is one of the most essential ways human beings learn how to communicate with each other and navigate their lives. For example, when one sees the octagonal stop sign ... even without the words being visible ... everyone knows and has accepted that this is a stop sign and will consequently stop some form of action. Hoffman and Blumer (1969) who coined the term set out three basic premises of the perspective:

1. Humans act toward things on the basis of the meanings they ascribe to those things.

2. The meaning of such things is derived from, or arises out of, the social interaction that one has with others and the society.

3. These meanings are handled in, and modified through, an interpretative process used by the person in dealing with the things he/she encounters.

This belief system does not have to be factual. Therefore, in some ways, this model encompasses mostly interpretations that can include perceptions of one another that can be oppressive. It can be a Justified True Belief as Gettier might argue (Lehrer, 2000). Meaning, if a group carries a particular belief and this group has enough members to be comprise a majority, then the truth that they believe can be justified, therefore, accepted.

In regards to African Americans, generally speaking, Symbolic Interactionism and Cooley's Looking Glass Self say that whatever constructed image represents "Blackness" and whatever meaning is attached to this Blackness comes from the social interaction that one has with others and society. As this Blackness is subjectively interpreted by others ... action is taken and directed by those meanings. As illustrated in Diagram 3, Symbolic Interactionism as an extension of the *Looking Glass Self* and a racist System reveals that the constructed Marginalized Black Male, peering into the mirrors held by Others outside of his own existence, perceives him as a thug, rapist, athlete, entertainer, minority, and so forth.

Some of these judgments may be true (based on specific events or individuals), while some of the judgments may be connected to *stereotypes* that are not true at all for this particular male. The main point is that the marginalized, Black Male is powerless over how others see him and he can only move *within the confines* of their perceptions, no further. The AA male must receive a "pass" or "permission" to move outside the constructs prescribed to him (Diagram 3).

Diagram 3. Cooley's Looking Glass Self of Oppression

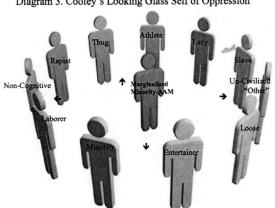

Until that *pass* is given, the African American Male will be viewed through the lens of one or more of these constructs.

The outside constructs that prohibit free movement of Self, what I call Prescribed Confining Constructs, are labels that are not necessarily chosen or regulated by the subject. Instead, individuals who have been conditioned and *socialized* to see Black Males in a particular way have chosen them. As defined by McQuail, the process of socialization should be viewed "as the teaching of established norms and values by ways of symbolic rewards and punishment for different kinds of behavior, and as the learning process whereby we all learn how to behave in certain situations and learn the expectations which go with a given role or status in society (Zoonen, p. 51, 1994)."

In other words, if I think Black males are violent and up to no good, when I encounter them, I will treat them as such. The Black Males, in turn, will attempt to navigate from this projected perception. So, not only are they marginalized in general, the African American male is forced to navigate through and around these constructs of perception on a daily basis. "Driving While Black" is a good example of this form of oppression.

The lines that border their existence, systemically, are comprised of the views of others that serve to support the strength and power structure of others. So, to make others feel comfortable, the African American male has to prove he is not a rapist before he is judged differently. He has to prove that he is not a thug or he is more than an athlete. He has to prove that he can't dance like the stereotypical Black Male can before he is viewed differently ... different from the racist infrastructure that exists in this county. Because the Black Male is confined to this limiting navigational process and process of validation and justification, I argue, that the Black Male is not truly free to be his *authentic self*, let alone free to be *actively* masculine. This process is selectively and methodically disempowering the Black Male. The conflict is inevitable.

There is a fear of saying the obvious ... that racism does exist because most people don't want to be called a racist. But, this fear must be addressed because the voice of the African American individual, even scholar is silenced, omitted or marginalized from important dialogues ... hence a form of micro-invalidation. The night that Trayvon Martin was murdered is the night where the *Looking Glass Self*, Symbolic Interactionism and Marginalization through the prism of racism collided. I will speak briefly about some of the coverage of this case and then I will move on to the solution. George Zimmerman, due to his lack of or limited experience with Black Males over the age of 10, judged Trayvon through the lens of what a black, criminal, "punk" looked like, *symbolically*. It is one thing to not be intimidated by young 5 and 8 year- old little black boys versus not being intimidated by young teenage Black men[7]. Zimmerman's judgment was clouded. That night, Trayvon was nothing more than a constructed prototype that provokes negativity and fear encased in the color of Blackness and he was judged accordingly, rather than the content of his character. So, George Zimmerman, who I propose, already harbored a fear of the Black

Male, felt that his life was in danger (ironically as a result of putting Trayvon's life in danger), shot and killed Trayvon. And, he was found not guilty. Not unlike the days of slavery. This process of intentional or unintentional or even incognizant racism played out in the courtroom as well.

It is my position that the White prosecutors were not able to represent Martin, to the fullest extent of the law, because not only did they not allow race to enter into the argument, which was the most central theme and element that contributed to Trayvon's death, but because they, themselves, were viewing and analyzing this crime through the lens of Whiteness. I propose that these lawyers share the same fears as other White Americans (including Zimmerman) who engage in incognizant or intentional racism. For example, this process of the trifecta racist and oppressive module I have explained (Marginalization, *Looking Glass Self,* Symbolic Interactionism) exhibited itself in the fact that, numerous times during the trial, George Zimmerman was described as a "good guy" who made a terrible mistake … positioning Zimmerman, subliminally, in a positive light. This performance did three things. It allowed the already racist beliefs, incognizant or not, of the jury and public to: see them both as merely two kids/males who met at the wrong time and wrong place, equally; to quietly exhibit an understanding and acceptance of white racism and black fear that existed in the deep resonance of the attorneys and their connection to the non-black audience; and because the mention of race was not allowed to enter into the courtroom, it allowed a reasonable doubt to be planted into the minds of a group of people who cannot fathom the idea that someone, constructed as white like they are, would kill a person simply because of his race. I believe that the subconscious or conscious thinking of the White jurors and others was that, because they wouldn't and couldn't kill someone just because of their race, Zimmerman couldn't either. This allowed the disbelieving White person to rid him or herself of guilt in regards to racist tendencies and to also find him, not guilty. I also have to say that the mere fact that the element of Race was not allowed to enter the courtroom is an injustice in and of itself, generally-speaking. Not only is justice not served fairly, it allows acts of racism as well as racists to exist unchallenged. Consequently, unchallenged racist acts are also allowed to continue to destroy this country. Most, will plead and yell that they are not racist! Perhaps they are not. Or, perhaps they are guilty of incognizant racism.

Outside of the courtroom, literary "bullhorns" and exclusionary processes that speak to the masses support this System of incognizant racism. Heider defines incognizant racism as a phenomenon that "occurs when journalists produce news products day-in and day-out that simply exclude any meaningful coverage of racial-ethnic communities" (Heider, p. 52, 2000). It is unintentional. It is part of their schematic makeup that cannot be separated from the journalists, and I would add, media messengers, themselves. This is one of the reasons why stereotypical racist coverage of African Americans prevails in a ubiquitous way in all forms of media portrayals. Media and journalism processes play an important, supportive role in perpetuating the fear of

Blacks, African Americans, Black Americans. Much of the portrayals audience members see along these lines are actually fiction. For example, according to FBI data collection, the majority of racial hate crimes are overwhelmingly White on Black. But, this is not how it is portrayed in the media. Most of the time the audience views Black on White hate crimes, especially in "mainstream" news. This method of framing, perpetuates the ideology that White Americans should fear Black Americans, the same type of media propaganda that was used during times of slavery and challenged by the Social Responsibility Theory discussed in the 1947 Hutchins Commission and the findings of the 1967 Kerner Commission and Report.

Freedom of the press, however, allows the Framing theory to remain active within the hands of journalists who believe in, like I do, John Milton's Marketplace of Ideas. However, with this freedom comes accountability. For instance, in two separate opinion columns, *Washington Post* contributors, Richard Cohen and Kathleen Parker wrote arguments validating the fear Whites have of Blacks. Cohen writes,

> "Where is the politician who will own up to the painful complexity of the problem and acknowledge the widespread fear of crime committed by young black males? This does not mean that raw racism has disappeared, and some judgments are not the product of invidious stereotyping. It does mean, though, that the public knows young black males commit a disproportionate amount of crime. In New York City, blacks make up a quarter of the population, yet they represent 78 percent of all shooting

suspects — almost all of them young men. We know them from the nightly news. Those statistics represent the justification for New York City's controversial stop-and-frisk program, which amounts to racial profiling writ large. After all, if young black males are your shooters, then it ought to be young black males whom the police stop and frisk. Still, common sense and common decency, not to mention the law, insist on other variables such as suspicious behavior. Even still, race is a factor, without a doubt. It would be senseless for the police to be stopping Danish tourists in Times Square just to make the statistics look good. I wish I had a solution to this problem. If I were a young black male and were stopped just on account of my appearance, I would feel violated. If the police are abusing their authority and using race as the only reason, that has got to stop.

But if they ignore race, then they are fools and ought to go into another line of work[8]."

I propose Mr. Cohen's words speak to the theories of Constructed Whiteness and Framing. First, because he is attempting to understand the objective side of things (the Black side and the White side) with limited knowledge or credentials of the Black experience or what it is to be Black in America, his thoughts nullify each other in my opinion. For example, Mr. Cohen points out that in New York City, most of the violent crimes are committed by Black Males. However, in the United States of America, White Americans comprise the majority if individuals arrested for crime, including crimes of violence. White Americans lead in the category of forcible rape, tied with murder and non-negligent manslaughter, lead in aggravated assault, burglary, and so on[9]. In other words, by number, White Americans could be viewed and framed as more violent than Black Americans, in general, if I chose to frame it as such. With Hate Crimes, the same database from the FBI reveals that the majority of the offenders are White as well[10]. Most of the violent crimes committed by African American males occur in predominantly Black neighborhoods. And even if Mr. Cohen, a White Male, decided to venture into a Black neighborhood, statistics and research studies as far back as the Kerner Commission, reveal that he is pretty safe as a White person, unless, of course, he steps in the line of fire of a gang war. No one is safe in this type of environment. Although I appreciate Mr. Cohen's attempt to explain this complex, racial problem, because of the facts, I propose that his own fear, understanding and acceptance of the Black Male as someone violent, allowed him to attempt to speak with authority, even asserting that it is only "logical" to stop and frisk a Black Male. Cohen writes that, "if young black males are your shooters, then it ought to be young black males whom the police stop and frisk." Or young black males should be the ones pursued. Which is exactly what Zimmerman did. But, Zimmerman was wrong. The stereotype did not fit the individual and Trayvon Martin died because a logical "guess," his guess and assumption was wrong. The same sentiment that Zimmerman had the night he killed Martin, is the same type of sentiment that can grow from such hasty generalizations as made by Mr. Cohen in his column. We must be careful.

Strangely, in the same article Cohen

tries to relate to the Black Male experience by writing, "if I were a young black male and were stopped just on account of my appearance, I would feel violated. If the police are abusing their authority and using race as the only reason, that has got to stop. But if they ignore race, then they are fools and ought to go into another line of work.[11]" I find a few things problematic about his analyses. First, throughout his entire piece, he made no reference to why crime is so high in particular areas. If he did an investigation, he would find historical, economic and racist reasons in the cultural bricks that make up the crime-ridden areas. Second, in no way, can Mr. Cohen ever relate to the Black Male experience. Even in his imagination, he can only simply do that; imagine how it would feel to be a targeted Black Male. To feel violated, I will concede, he may be able to relate. But again, only on a small scale. Black Males are violated constantly in every day life. Their images are violated every single day. They are profiled in a negative way, every single day. They receive less pay because they are Black Males, every single day. They are wrongly shot and killed, racially profiled, demeaned, emasculated, every single day. So, unless Mr. Cohen has this type of experience from the day he is born to possibly the day he dies, not just in this country, but in the global world in general, no, Mr. Cohen, you cannot relate. But, thank you for trying.

Cohen writes that police should not stop a Black Male because of his race, but if they don't stop a Black Male because of his race, they should go into another line of work? So, this equation does not give the police any logical, acceptable alternative to racial profiling. I further argue that the equation itself is problematic for any group or individual, based on its premise. For example, using the same equation, if in fact, most spies who betray this country and its national security are White Males, would it be ok for me to follow Cohen's process of a hasty generalization and say that the American public should stop allowing White Males to hold high security jobs? Should I develop the belief and discriminatory action that because most pedophiles on record are White Males, they should not be allowed to adopt children under 18? Mostly White Males design bombs for mass destruction and terrorism. Most serial killers are White Males. Most of the Black people who will be killed because of the color of their skin will be killed by White Males. Most perpetuators of Ponzi schemes are White Males. The majority of snipers are White Males. Knowing these facts and others like them, should laws be passed to stop all White Males from, buying particular types of gunnery, serving in the military, being employed in highly classified positions? Should we then say that the police, bank officials, and people in general, especially African Americans, should be on the lookout for White Males in general? Is it acceptable for Law Enforcement officials to pull White Males over, ask them questions, and shoot them over 35 times because they reached for their wallet after they were racially profiled? Deter them from running for President of the United States because they can't be trusted? Should we not allow white people to hold financial positions or positions of currency? I should think not, because it is not fair and it is not logical. And our "guessing" could be wrong. We should make all attempts to judge EVERYONE, individually and by the content of their character. As absurd as the question I pose may sound, this is precisely the way Black Males; African American Males are profiled, daily. Just as geniuses can be a little crazy, "rational thinking" can be a bit ludicrous. I also find it a bit interesting that Mr. Cohen had to leave the country, rhetorically speaking, in order to make a comparison, writing, "It would be senseless for the police to be stopping Danish tourists in Times Square just to make the statistics look good."

At the end of my analysis, I ask myself why didn't Mr. Cohen question his own possible internalized "racism" in writing this article and taking the position he chose? Is the answer the same reason why he felt that it was ok to speak about racism without LIVING as a victim of racism for a justifiable period of time to even have such a voice? Could it be that he engaged in an act of "entitlement" that I spoke about in my discussions of Marginalization, *Looking Glass Self* and Symbolic Interactionism? Within the System, the fact that he was born in the majority, conditioned in the majority and thinks in the majority … he also postures himself to think for the minority as well. This is the way he has been conditioned and socialized. As so the oppression continues. I'm not saying that Mr. Cohen is intentionally practicing "entitlement" or that he is a racist. What *I am saying* is that because he boldly speaks from a social location that is indigenous of the perspective of the Black victim, is problematic. I appreciate Mr. Cohen's attempts. I really do. But I cannot agree with his assessments completely. However, behind every stereotype, and even fear, there is a bit of truth, which gives some credence to his allegations, which I will expound on, momentarily. Before I move on, here's just a thought. If we racially profiled White Males, how many crimes and elements of injustice would be stopped? Since white people make up the majority of the population, which also means, the majority of offenders by sheer numbers, would there be less crime in the U.S. and global wars? Perhaps. Still, I submit and will argue, that racially profiling as a way to control and monitor a group is problematic, whether the focus is on one group or all groups.

Mr. Cohen's writing colleague, Kathleen Parker, wrote similar analyses. I had a problem with a point she made when she wrote, "the point is that this is one of those rare instances in which everyone is right within his or her own experience. African Americans are right to perceive that Martin was followed because he was black, but it is wrong to presume that recognizing a racial characteristic is necessarily racist." Recognizing a racial characteristic doesn't mean that this act of recognition is not racist? To pass judgment about someone based on that person's race is not racist? How does this make sense? Either way I turn and twist it; it is still a racist gesture. Here's what I think the problem is with this. Everyone assumes that being called a "racist" always implies something bad or negative or vicious, even abnormal. I don't believe this is the case. Whether a racist notion is good or bad would depend on the action that proceeds and in part of this racially induced judgment. If you have a belief or attitude about someone or a group and it is based on race, it is racist. This is how Symbolic Interactionism operates. If you carry out an action connected to this belief that is negative, it is discriminatory racism. But, the philosophical question of what is and isn't acceptable as a definition and connotation of 'racist'is debatable. I do have a question for Ms. Parker, however. How is it that White People are the sole authorities on what is racist and who is racist? What extensive qualifications do they have? Do they wake up and think about their color and wonder if they will be pulled over or shot and killed because of their race? Let me make my point in another way. After seeing someone punch someone else, if you wanted to know whether or not it hurt, would you ask the *receiver* of the punch or the one who threw the punch? If you wanted to know if the wife abused the husband, would you ask the wife who may have performed the abuse or the husband who received the alleged abusive treatment? So, if you wanted to know if a certain act was racist or not, would you ask the receiver of the attack or the perpetrator? Or would you perhaps ask someone who has a history of knowledge of racist acts, first hand, such as White and Jewish civil rights activists? Although, as a collective, White Americans are not usually on the receiving end of racism because they navigate their lives within a primarily white environment-by default, ironically, they, somehow comprise the long list of experts and authorities on the race problem itself. I find this baffling. I'm not focusing on Ms. Parker when I say this. I'm basically referring to the media images and spokespersons found on networks today. Again, perhaps this acts as an example of entitlement within the System. Nonetheless, we can all agree that we cannot know someone's heart, therefore, in some cases, their motives. I appreciate her attempt to talk about the issue. In order to address the real problem of racism, I believe that the voices of individuals like Cohen and Parker are needed. However, I do not believe, that they, or any aggregate that is primarily and overwhelmingly white, must always lead the discussions or the solutions. Enlightened white and black individuals as well as other people of color should always be a part of these important discourses.

Acts of incognizant racism and schematic influence by way of "framing" reaches not only the media outlets, but also the perspectives of individuals who are not journalists. Reflecting back to the aforementioned case, Zimmerman, for example, is suing NBC for the way he says he was inaccurately portrayed as a racist. Because of the time constraints that are innate in broadcast journalism, a decision to edit the 9-1-1 audio recording was made.

The result led listeners to believe George Zimmerman mentioned Trayvon's race without provocation, when in fact, initially, the dispatcher asked Zimmerman the race of Trayvon. *That was the first time.* What was *not* mentioned and what Zimmerman *has not* answered is the question of why he mentioned Trayvon's race again, later in the tape at 1:19 in the recording *without provocation.* Furthermore, the 9-1-1 transcript also reveals Zimmerman's fear and inaccurate portrayal of Trayvon with more than 20 descriptors. In order:

1. Suspicious

2. Up to no good

3. On drugs or something

4. Dark hoodie

5. Staring at me

6. Staring at me

7. Looking at houses

8. Coming towards me

9. Hand in waistband

10. Black male

11. Button on shirt

12. Something's wrong with him

13. Coming to check me out

14. What is his deal?

15. Something in his hands

16. Assholes always getting away

17. He's running

18. Following him

19. He ran

20. Don't know where the kid is

Because of the way George framed Trayvon that rainy night and the way Trayvon was allowed to be framed in court that excluded the Black elephant in the room-the element of race - Trayvon was never portrayed or judged or approached as a victim that night, nor during the trial. His position of viewing the peculiar automobile following him, as a weapon, was not even entered into the discourse. So Trayvon, innocent of any wrong doing that night, was killed that night and then again in court because George Zimmerman's fear, consequently, his actions as well, were deemed justifiable. The same fear that resonates with so many White people *and some Black people* of the image and reality of "Bad Boys" who are Black, permitted Zimmerman's actions, judgment and decision to pursue and, subsequently, kill Trayvon were viewed and accepted as reasonable and a shadow of a doubt was casted within the minds of the jury. An innocent young man who was, initially, passive, who, like any one else in a similar position, feared for his life because someone he did not know, was pursuing him when he was not breaking any law, had no gun, and was not on drugs. Unfortunately, he was also not allowed to be frightened or simply defend himself and live another day. All of this occurred, I propose, not because Zimmerman is a bad guy. It occurred because Zimmerman was allowed to think in a constructed racist manner that was derived from a corrupt System of being, thinking, and judging. Zimmerman, like so many others, was conditioned to fear someone who looked just like Trayvon that night. Trayvon just happened to be the target, this time.

CHAPTER 4
The "Black" American Issue

The problem with racial profiling did not begin with the murder of 18 year-old Michael Brown, 17 year-old Trayvon Martin … or the murder of 22 year-old Oscar Grant III … or the murder of 17 year-old Jordan Davis … or even the murder of 14 year-old Emmitt Till. It began during slavery, with the reconstruction of the Black Male's Image of Power and Competence into images of being weak, incompetent, uncivilized, dangerous, and violent and should be feared. It was a power move that gave one aggregate power, while disempowering the other. This power, however, was intensified, made stronger by Black Americans, themselves. As I stated earlier, behind every fear and stereotype, there is some truth. The negative images of Blackness as violent, uncivilized, and immoral criminals is based on the fact that some people are just that way, both, Black people and White people. Some Black Americans do bad things. However, the negative images of this type of Blackness is allowed to prevail and move to the forefront, representing **all Black people**, in general, and Black Males, specifically. Because some Black people do bad things and the resulting images and stories are allowed to permeate media messages in an imbalanced way that conveys them as being the main criminals in society, there is a small semblance of validity to Ms. Parker and Mr. Cohen's fears. If I received messages from society, media, educators, politicians and relatives to fear Black people for most of my life, I probably would, especially if I lived a monolithic life that lacked diversity. Sometimes, we do have choices. But, I propose there is something just as if not more dangerous going on. That as a result of being mistreated and misrepresented and disrespected for hundreds of years, Black Americans have become confused, angry, and just down right tired of being Black in America. It began with implementation of the institution of Slavery and the predicaments it put White and Black people in that we have yet to escape. When non-Blacks look at African Americans from this country or abroad[12], they are either going to view you/me/us as present day slaves or descendants of slaves. The common denominator is the constructed image of what a slave looks like and whatever follows. Slavery continues to be a part of our image, our history and our unique element of Symbolic Interactionism. In order to fully understand the System, how it works and how you can move through it, you must embrace this valuable fact, yes. However, I strongly encourage you to embrace it in a way that moves you from the margins. Slavery in America is only a small piece of what we are, who we are and how we came to be. We are the offspring of the strongest of the strong whose ancestors survived ... and our people are much older than 250 years. We must review and revisit our Identity from the root up.

Bradley (1996) states that there are two types of identity, the Personal and the Social. The Personal makes up our core psychology while the Social explains and dictates how we locate ourselves in society. Using mixed methodologies, ten years of my empirical and theoretical research has focused on the socialization of leadership and self empowerment by examining the design of power <u>within the constructs</u> in which people live, work and learn as well as image portrayals in the media[13]. Some of my findings on race and leadership development reveal that while an African American can have a strong Personal Identity displaying high levels of Self Esteem, they carry low performances of confidence and Transformational leadership styles within particular social and professional settings. This relates to their Social Identity. An example of this phenomenon ... at predominantly White universities, when I studied African American journalism students who held leadership role positions in classroom and newsroom settings[14], they tested high on Rosenberg's self esteem scale but failed to perform their duties with confidence. Following observation analysis and in-depth interviews, I learned that this occurred because they didn't feel as if they were treated as equals and if they pushed their power onto their White classmates, they would be ostracized ... even feeling that their work would be sabotaged because no one would want to work with them if they were too pushy. The responses from their White classmates corroborated this fear with statements like, "as long as they get along with us, we'll get along with them." So, although the African American students held positions of authority and power, because of the racist filter they were viewed through, their Social Self remained in a position of marginalization and disempowerment[15].

Results from another quantitative study I conducted on the image portrayals of White, Black, Hispanic and Asian Americans in prime time commercials, five networks for five consecutive days, revealed that African Americans had low representation when it came to leadership roles, major speaking roles, cognitive aptitude, images of family, and economic prosperity.[16] Additionally, in 1084 commercials, not one Asian American female spoke one single word! To the audience members who lack diversity, the repetitive viewing of these images and role portrayals may say that African Americans don't and/or can't lead and Asian American women have nothing to say. As we all know, both of these messages are untrue, inaccurate and problematic. Nonetheless, via media outlets, these designed images continue to reach into our homes and possibly our psyche, subliminally, continuously challenging us to be clear as to who we are. When I asked my Chinese colleagues if this omission bothered them, the fact that not one Asian woman spoke in over one thousand commercials, they said that they didn't mind at all because they have a rich culture in China. The image portrayal in the Western media was for Americans, not them. Their responses makes obvious, the importance of having a cultural foundation outside of America.

From athletic to political, a plethora of examples of cognitive and behavioral slavery can be found in the media. It is important to examine and challenge media and their role in this process because media convey messages to this country and the WORLD about who you are as a people, what is beautiful, handsome and acceptable and the connotations of what is Black and African American. As a result of some of these media messages, males and females, black and white, pay millions upon millions of dollars to change our bodies, calves, noses, "pecs," posterior derrieres, and the list goes on.

It is my belief that one of the essential elements of Self-Esteem and the freedom to be happy, is the belief that it is *the differences* and the loving and acceptance of *these differences* that can make this country and the world, so beautiful. So, Asian Americans should not be forced to change the direction of the slant outlining their beautiful eyes. People of color should not be encouraged or feel pressure to take part in dangerous feats of bleaching their skin so that they become a different color. People should not be forced or feel compelled to sit in the sun for dangerous periods of time just to change the beauty of their white skin, or other procedures to change the thinness of their lips. Just being yourself should be acceptable and encouraged because the true meaning of America is the belief that aggregates are allowed to exist in this country without losing their own identity. But, we have become a culture of change ... change from who we are naturally, to something or someone we are unnaturally not. Haven't we?

The media not only teaches aesthetic lessons, media also plays a role in teaching and conditioning African Americans, Black Americans how to act, what to think of themselves, and what others should think of us. This part of the process is extremely dangerous because being unaware of the negative subliminal messages prohibits an AA to act on a conscious level that challenges the stereotypes. It is too deep within the AA's psyche for them to even know that they are doing it. Because the majority deems these images and roles as acceptable, AAs internalize this marginalized agenda and moved towards a self-fulfilling prophecy that is dictated by others. So, African Americans *become* the negative image that is set forth and are rewarded for doing so. This practice and process is continuous and constant with mutual participation, consciously or subconsciously.

Previous research studies reveal that African Americans, for example, are primarily portrayed in stereotypical roles: entertainers, comedians, criminals and athletes. In other words, African Americans have historically received passes to perform in ways that entertain or perpetuate fear, and the image portrayals follow. Present day, unfortunately, there has been little change. To have a career in the entertainment business is not a bad thing and if someone commits a crime, people should know about it and even what the suspect looks like. The problem is, these images are usually the *majority of image* portrayals one witnesses of African Americans on a constant basis in the media. In mainstream media, we don't see the present day African American heroes such as Leroy W. Homer who crashed his plane in Philadelphia to save the lives of innocent people during the 9-11 attacks or one of the co-developers of the Gamma Electric Cell that enables the use of cell phones, Henry Sampson, Jr. Instead, we see a White American male in the role of Homer in the 2006 movie, United 93, and no mention of Sampson, Jr. at all ... that is, unless you read *Essence* or *Jet*, or *Ebony* or any other Black-focused publication. Most, non-African Americans do not, which is also one of the reasons we have such a lack of diversity in this country and a lack of understanding and knowledge of the many developments African Americans have contributed to the prosperity of this country. There are no real heroes or "sheroes" image portrayals of African Americans outside of the non-threatening stereotypes on a constant basis. So, again, the System allows this to happen. Consequently, the perpetual nullification by omission positions African Americans, as an aggregate, not to be respected nor viewed as credible contributors to the American way by audience members ... including other African Americans.

Other examples of micro-aggressive racism include the recent Don Sterling debacle that says, you can play with them, hire them, have intimate and personal relationships with them, but never really be the friend of an African American. Even the fact that a mostly White Male power structure is now dictating a dress code to African American adult male athletes as if they are children, is troubling. But, in some way, I get it. If you want your players to be role models representing a particular image, then perhaps a dress code is warranted. It is a business. However, it can be problematic when viewed within the framework of a racist System. The complexity of this conundrum is obvious.

Individuals of the "White" construct who have a lack of diversified understanding will usually engage in stereotypical prejudices. This process is exacerbated if they are on the receiving end of distorted and imbalance image portrayals of African Americans/Black Americans. These individuals of the System perform in very distinct ways, consciously or subconsciously. In other words, they have bought into the System. They view all Blacks as being: less intelligent, lazy, from Harlem or predominantly Black neighborhoods, abnormally violent and aggressive and poor. They also believe Black people only listen to 'Black' music. White people who operate within this System will not marry a Black person because of what *Others* (meaning White people) will think of them. They will marry, however, an African. They will not move into predominantly Black neighborhoods nor, willingly, attend predominantly Black schools and institutions even though this would make education more affordable for some. In the academy and in general social settings, they, and their children refuse to address professional Black Americans by their official titles such as Dr., Professor, or Attorney. In the academic realm, they don't push Black students academically because they have a deep belief that Black children are less intelligent. In these situations, a teacher/professor will fail Black students rather than work with them or they will give the Black students high marks, pushing them through the system, setting the Black student up to eventually fail in the future in some capacity. Constructed White physicians and dentists of this System will offer stereotypical treatment to Black patients without proper testing or patient history. While they say anyone of any race can be called a 'Nigger,' this is mostly theoretical because they mainly use the label for Black people. If they use this racial slur to label others, the targets have some connection to Black people or the Black culture such as biracial individuals, White individuals whose social system is mostly Black or dark skinned people not of the Black race such as some Mexicans and Polynesians (as examples). The exception to this rule consists of labels directed at particular White individuals. White individuals who are viewed as a disgrace or embarrassment to the White constructed race are usually called 'White trash' or in rare instances, 'White Nigger.' White Americans who are derivatives of the System also engage in unfair practices in housing, employment, and consumerism.

Because this embedded System of racism has been around for a long time (read the words of Confederate Vice President Alexander Stephens), its influence is not only ubiquitous … at times, it can be downright unsettling. After using slurs such as "nappy headed hoes" an individual is allowed to continue to have a voice, just from a different platform, a bigger platform (Don Imus). We are killed when we run for help and knock on the door of an unsuspecting household that is not used to seeing "us," much less in the stillness of the dark (Renisha McBride). AAs are killed when they play their music too loud for another (Michael Dunn). They are mis-identified on national television (Samuel Jackson), even mis-identified as a criminal when attempting to get inside of our own home within our own neighborhood (Dr. Henry Louis Gates, Jr.) … and if a mature, adult, African American Male who happens to be a Harvard professor is insulted by the way he is being treated, and rightly so, this MAN will be arrested as the BOY he is perceived to be.

Then there is the Black side of buying into the System. One of the damaging results of this form of racist micro-aggression is Internalized Colonization and Racial Fatigue. Evidence of this occurring is observed in the continuously growing development of African Americas engaging in the practice of self-hate; hatred of their own people and race. We also engage in the practice of emulating and assimilating, simultaneously, in order to be accepted into this racist and oppressive structure that we do not and should not want to belong to entirely. After hundreds and hundreds of years of trying to change who we are on the inside as well as on the outside, after constantly trying to finally feel a sense of acceptance, validity, equality ... the constant, intense, silently tortured efforts of our desperate need to feel wanted and loved by others has finally begun to turn on us. We are finally imploding and exploding and giving everyone reasons to NOT want to be us, to want to fear us, hate us, be like us-but not us, even to the point where we, ourselves, don't like or even love ourselves or being Black. For example, in some extreme cases, some of us who are Black/African Americans don't/ won't identify as such. Suddenly, we want to be called just Americans, like the identifiers, Black or African American, hold the power of a scarlet letter of disgrace. I believe this occurs for three reasons. One reason is because we have been conditioned to be ashamed of the African side of ourselves in return for an *imaginary* successful assimilation process. A second reason is because we have no knowledge of our African side and we want to be in the "In-Group" not the "Out-Group." However, I assert that after investigating our genealogical roots outside of American, many of us will learn that what we believe are *American* mores and traditions or elements connected to our family, are actually *African* ways or ways of our ancestors *as well* as our American ways. The final reason I believe claiming to be nothing more than American is problematic is because, fundamentally, this is not reality. By claiming we are just American, at this juncture, would imply that we have all of the rights and privileges of a White, male, heterosexual, American. We know that this is not the case. On one hand, I hope we can all one day simply say that we are just American. On the other hand, would it be so bad to claim both one's ancestral and national identities? Perhaps, the answer to this question will continue to be a personal choice. I think the more important question lies in the *reasoning* behind the choices. Regardless of the decisions, personal choices are acts of freedom so I support the process.

Other forms of Internalized Colonization and Racial Fatigue are present when African Americans/Black Americans join in the berating of each other for attributes we may not be able to control naturally instead of loving the person and being proud (racist comments about Gabby Douglas' hair). We allow others to call us "Nigger" (Paris Hilton, popular entertainers, etc.) and stop protesting even when individuals who deliver racist rants receive contracts for more episodes and a new spin-off show, as they continue to target individuals of color on the program (Dog the Bounty Hunter). Although a person has admitted to positioning light skinned ones in the front of the restaurant and the dark skinned ones in the kitchen, we say that she is not a racist and we forgive her (Paula Deen).

And some of us go even further by asking her to work with young Black Males before proving herself to be a positive influence to these young men. We allow others to say they are sorry and go through a sensitivity course of some sort, or even have a beer with us on a grassy lawn, and all is well. Forgiveness is great. However, forgiveness of the Truth is even better. It allows people to be loved right where they are so that there can be change or so that that person can be held accountable for their mis-step. It also allows the complaints of AAs a sense of validity. But, how can we be upset about such attacks, when we, ourselves, are joining in? When we, ourselves, have bought into the System? Within the most ubiquitous forms of media (music and television), we call each other "Niggahs," "Hoes," Bitches and engage in physical fights and make billions upon billions of dollars from engaging in such self-destruction (reality programs[17]). With our permission, we are allowing the hurt and pain and suffering of being Black and/or Poor to be *exploited* on national television without receiving any attention or compassion for the central problem-the breakdown of the Black family and its people. What other aggregate does this? What other aggregate makes BILLIONS of dollars by demeaning their own people? In the entertainment business, we constantly worry about crossing over when others don't feel or echo these same desires nor give the Black culture of yesterday and today proper credit for the influence used in making them the success stories they are today. Businesses continue to make money from AAs, in AAs neighborhoods, yet, fail to put money *back* into this same neighborhood … an act that will directly help improve the condition of its people. A slave continues to think that they need validation and acceptance from his or her oppressor. Do we engage in this type of process? Think about it. Can you now see the slave mentality I am speaking of, now? And African Americans who project their frustration and anger and hurt and pain in negative and violent ways are simply exacerbating the problem. Killing, robbing, or hurting someone because you are angry is never acceptable. We, African Americans, continue to engage in gang wars and drug wars where we are killing our own people. So, no, this is not a White problem. And the list of such examples grows on a daily basis.

But, we must also ask ourselves, why is this violence occurring? What is the root of the problem? If someone states that the problem is simply the "person," they are missing the big picture. Again, I strongly assert that killing individuals, innocent or not, is not acceptable, ever. However, the problem is simply not what it seems. I would argue that one of the reasons these types of heinous acts that make innocent victims targets occur is because the perpetrators, themselves, are victims as well. They are victims of a racist, classist, sexist System that has bullied them, their mothers and fathers, grandmothers and grandfathers, etc. for generations. Furthermore, their viewpoint from the margins is narrowly focused, therefore, they look to the *individuals* rather than the real problem[18]. The target should be the System itself. Legitimately and justifiably so, African Americans have become tired and fatigued from fighting racism on a daily basis. We have become tired and fatigued from just simply being BLACK. And what happens when you're tired? You become careless. You begin to make serious mistakes that you can't take back.

We are destroying ourselves, one by one, for the entire world to see. Although racism may have begun this revolution, it is not solely a White problem. But, everyone American, regardless of race, must understand the condition of being Black in America because it is America that built this racist-discriminatory System. It is the racist System, supported and designed from social, racial, gender and class injustice from the beginning that is the culprit. And it is this same System that continues to protect and support some of its leaders and their/ our mistakes as well. This System that allows injustices to prevail should be challenged by all, and challenged constantly, joint-by-joint, until a better, more effective, fair and balanced, system is built.

CHAPTER 5
The "African" American Issue

When we speak of the Sociology of Self, we are referring to the "I" and "Me" Identity and Subjectivity. Identity is about belonging. It's about what you have in common with some people and what differentiates you from others. At its most basic level, identity gives a person a sense of personal location, the stable core to individuality. It is also about your social relationships and your complex involvement with others. The three main arguments of Identities is that we are born with them, they are culturally and historically dependent and fluid and fragmented, and are a result of conscious and unconscious thought and emotion (Bradley, 1996). During the 60s, there was a strong Black Identity prevalent in America. The "say it loud, I'm black and I'm proud" chants flowing from the nearest radio or stereo, landed on the streets of Harlem and other predominantly black neighborhoods, as well as within average households. It was Black Pride that dictated a walk, a pimp or lean in our walk, a swagger that leaned to the left as our Afros flowed in the wind and shielded us from the sun. We were proud to be black, a Black American that was self-defined and connected to our African roots. The problem for African Americans is that after the flames of the Black Power Movement died to a smoldering ember, our Personal and

Social identity became unstable and dictated by others. Much of this, I would argue, is due to the nullification of who we are as a people and as an Identity *before* American slavery and who we are as complete Americans post-slavery. This is a form of micro-invalidation that is perpetuated and sustained by the System.

African Americans continue, unsuccessfully in most situations, to try and assimilate and emulate a particular White construct because as far as we can see, in this country, or even parts of the world, there aren't any real positive benefits of being Black, pragmatically-speaking. This inductive form of reasoning is the result of being conditioned by the System. Neither African Americans nor White Americans are taught lessons of a Black Legacy, an African Legacy. We know of the White legacy and history, domestic and abroad, because the System (that includes the Media), teaches us this information, daily. Earlier in this paper, I discussed the limited and selective information that the System is teaching us, and others, about the Black American. The goals and images are not the same. African Americans have no or very little knowledge of their ancestral beginnings. They do not hold this knowledge base of historical facts nor is it taught to us or other aggregates on a consistent basis. So, can you really just blame the individual, who is a product of the System, for having certain prejudices and beliefs? African Americans and their sense of Self is incomplete because they are missing half of their Identity.

Because African Americans have been disconnected from their ancestral roots, there is no culturally-racially strong, positive, uplifting, foundation directed and maintained as they move through American society. **This form of oppression is indigenous of the AA cultural image and reality.** Furthermore, I believe this lack of legacy has made African Americans extremely vulnerable and weak in some ways. It's one thing to be an American, even a Black American, who is still treated as less than, less American. It's another thing to be *African American* and totally removed from your people that existed before slavery. From my previous studies and conference presentations and workshops, one aspect of Self-identification that was constantly absent was the obvious omission of fifty percent of an African American's African identity and heritage. Presentation after presentation, none of the African Americans in attendance could offer any specifics as to their African side. This is a clear and obvious form of Marginalization because the African American's identity remains located only in the position of subjugation, slavery. This limited construct of Identity is allowed to comprise the parameters of who and what an African American is by the System and by other African Americans. But, it is extremely important to know who you are and where you are socially located by Identity. I propose that for the African American, this identity must extend beyond the borders of slavery and America. But, it appears, some AAs may not agree.

Harvard professor and Director of Harvard's W.E.B. DuBois Institute for African and African American Research, Dr. Henry Louis Gates, Jr., is the preeminent leader of DNA genealogy for Americans, especially African Americans through mediated messages. It's not just Gates who is interested in bloodlines and social location, however. Due to advancement in technology, millions of records followed by at least that many inquiries happen everyday over the Internet. According to their website, Ancestry.com has "over 24 million family trees on its website," NBC produces specials and series about blood lines, such as, "Who do you think you are?," and the number of attendees at the Annual Genealogy Fair hosted by the National Archives in Washington, D.C. grows each year by the thousands. For years, Gates, has produced a line of PBS series on DNA testing: "Faces of America, African American Lives," and "Finding Your Roots with Henry Louis Gates, Jr." Famous celebrities like Meryl Streep, Rep. John Lewis-D. Ga., Stephen Colbert, Barbara Walters, Oprah Winfrey, with the assistance of Dr. Gates, found out about their roots, their slave masters, and their stories before an audience of over 25 million interested viewers. What's interesting is what these celebrities were mostly moved by. In a Washington Post article that focused on the 4th year of airing of one of his specials, Gates stated that "When I started the series, I thought the moving moment for my guests, in the case of the African American ones, would be when I revealed what tribe they came from in Africa, but it wasn't. It was revealing the names of slave ancestors. People would cry (Williams, 2012)." I propose that these strong emotions that emerged when the African American celebrities ingested the enslavement portion of their heritage illustrates my point of the partnered identity of African American and slave. Gates goes on to say, "nobody cried when I told them what tribe they came from in Africa. They were intellectually fascinated but not emotionally engaged, as when you're looking at your great-great-grandparents and they were slaves (Williams, 2012)." I think educational psychologist, Kadia Koroma, said it best when she said, "you can't mourn for someone you do not know." Like most African Americans, the participants in Dr. Gates' series had no *real* connection or even small connection with their African Ancestral roots or their people. Therefore, they could not relate to the loss of their African heritage nor the disconnect between them and their ancestral people. What is also troubling is that none of the celebrities thought to delve into the African side of their existence as a way of healing and moving from the margins. At least, that is the appearance disseminated as well as described by Gates, himself. I assert that there is something bigger and deeper going on here - a condition or phenomenon of loss and an incompleteness that should be and needs to be addressed. What is also interesting is that it appeared that the White Americans appeared to have the same emotional reactions when their families' connection to slavery was revealed as well. If their family members were slave owners, they were emotional. If they were not, they were still emotional.[19] I would posit that these reactions reveal *their connection* to the System as victims as I stated earlier. Just as important, the emotional reactions from both aggregates on the subject of slavery exemplify the need for the two races to come together for healing purposes.

There was one noticeable difference found within the process that I believe is worth mentioning. While there was a commonality between the aggregate along the lines of race in America, the White Americans had another history that they were just as interested in outside of America. The pursuit of their "total" identity, I propose, gives them a feeling of completeness. As Gates pointed out, the African Americans were not really interested in visiting their African ancestral locations, their identities outside of America. I believe their lack of interest is due to the enormous pain of the tortures of slavery that they have yet to reconcile as well as Internalized Colonization and Racial Fatigue. I also assert that because they did not move to find an element of healing in their ancestral roots, they remain incomplete and only partially healed, if at all.

In analyzing this work of genealogy and celebrity lineage, I believe an interesting juxtaposition occurred. While the African American celebrities who participated in this process are in financial positions to transgress negative stereotypes and possess social and economic mobility, they could not escape the internalized feeling of oppression associated with slavery. It is an effective illustration of the celebrity's own cognitive captivity of enslavement. In other words, because the System operates from the original premise of African Americans being slaves, and the African American has internalized this ideology, it is more important and valuable as to who you are in relation to your American slave background rather than your African background. A hypothetical example of this would be the court case of Oprah Winfrey taking on the state of Texas and Mad Cow's disease. In front of millions of people, Oprah faced the all-white, male cattle businessmen, was tried and won the case. She is elated as she steps out of the courtroom full of victory when someone steps in front of her and calls her a "Nigger." Immediately she is depressed and is no longer the billionaire who was able to transgress over multiple obstacles. She is unable to get back to "normal," emotionally because, above all else, deep down inside of her, she is trapped inside a constructed Self that views herself as having a blood connection only to slavery and the word "Nigger" that is often used. She feels that this pejorative slur holds some validity because of how she, like so many other African Americans who find themselves in a similar situation, has been conditioned and socialized. They have been conditioned and socialized to believe that there is nothing more to them, no other social location but Up or Down from Slavery. I would argue quite the contrary. I would argue that this is only one small, but important, element that makes up who we are as African Americans. I would also argue that within the ancestral roots found abroad, is, precisely, the location I believe the re-education and healing of Black America can take place … in the place of re-defining Self, the Situated Self (Berger, 1963 & Berger, Luckman, 1967).

It is across the borders, outside of the United States, that African Americans can begin to regain what was lost or taken from their sense of Self during the Middle Passage or other treks that led to slavery and oppression. Other Americans have a sense of belonging or knowing what group they belong to that does not relegate itself to slavery or an institution of only being oppressed and repressed. Most racial and ethnic dualities of identification have been able to survive here in the United States because of their immigrant status and origins. Irish-Americans, Italian-Americans, Hispanic/Latino Americans, Asian Americans, and European-Americans, even individuals of the Jewish faith, for example, have some known history of life before they came to the US.[20] When asked about their heritage, most individuals from each of these groups were able to tell me the origins of their family line, what their native language was, their original names, their foods, religion, music, mores, rituals, even traditions. There are Jewish holidays, Irish Pubs, "Little Italy" and "Chinatowns" the country over. These groups have a history, a heritage, and therefore, a legacy. Where is the African side of the cultural identity for African Americans? Other than what came out of slavery, what were we allowed to create, and keep (outside of Gullah), that sustains our connection to our African ancestors? Is it ok to wear a Dashiki to work? African attire and wardrobe and hairstyles? Probably not. Were we allowed to keep and practice our native language, food and diet, medicinal aptitudes and remedies, or spiritual and religious foundations? In the majority of cases, this was not allowed. So, here in the United States of America, there is a culturally, ethnically, racially disconnect among African Americans and the Global Identity that other aggregates do not have to address. This is an important distinction between immigrants on all levels and the African American whose African ancestors were brought over as slaves.

There have been attempts to rebuild this connection, but within the System, African Americans are viewed differently, unjustly and unfairly. When Black Americans attempt to support Black-owned businesses, for example, like other aggregates do when they buy from White-owned, Asian-owned, etc., businesses, they are called racists. This is occurring with the Empowerment Experiment lead by Maggie Anderson and her husband, John. When I go to a grocery store, it is a white-owned grocery store. The bank where I, and my white neighbors, conduct our financial transactions is white-owned. The gas station where we get our gas, white-owned. Following the deductive reasoning bestowed on African Americans, should we then be able to logically say that, from my choices, I am supporting white businesses? As to the White Americans who frequent these same establishments, should we say that they are racists because they conduct their businesses with only white-owned establishments? Why is it that when Black Americans are told to pull themselves up by their bootstraps, unless their bootstraps are located in white establishments, they are labeled racists? Is this fair? Is this just? Is it even proper reasoning? If you add in the business and financial support Systems that support these operations, discriminately, you can understand how deep the slave mentality reaches, on both sides. So, while we see other aggregates continue to succeed as groups, socially, politically, and economically, the African American aggregate is oppressed and splintered. It is how the System, as it is now, works.

Unlike African Americans during the 60s and prior, there is no common connection to a larger message of Blackness except with the connection to the institution of slavery within the states. What this means is that, unlike other races, Black people, African Americans don't move as a collective. Whatever positive movement up the social stratus that is made by a member of the African American culture, does not necessarily translate into positive movement as a group. We see examples of this in the case of Oprah Winfrey, President Barack Obama, Tyler Perry, Lee Daniels, Colin Powell, and Audra McDonald type situations; individuals whose achievements have the potential to transform the negative image of what it is to be African American or Black. These individuals have been quite successful, but their individual success was not Transformational ... their achievements did not translate into *African Americans* being viewed as productive, success-inclined, entrepreneurial type individuals. This is a cognitive process that is contrary to the way the images of other racial and ethnic aggregates are developed and sustained.

By now, we are all aware of examples of constructed Whiteness that carries the Ideology of White being good, positive, strong, intelligent, etc., beginning with the constructed image of "Jesus" and America's founding fathers. The plethora of White male roles models portrayed as the epitome of American success and intelligence leads and sustains this Ideology. Research studies have revealed that White children in schools, especially White males, for example, are thought of as intelligent, natural-born leaders until they prove themselves differently. This type of prototype processing occurs in other groups such as the Chinese. In some cases, Chinese and Chinese American students are automatically thought to be extremely intelligent in math and science not because they study harder and longer than most other groups, but because they are Chinese.

We know that not all individuals of Chinese descent are made the same, but the prototype/stereotype usually prevails. So a Chinese individual will be viewed with respect to the group's attributes. The attributes associated with these groups are positive attributes that others aspire to, placing them on a higher rung of the social stratus and away from the margins. This form of judgment and cognitive thinking through prototype processing does not occur within the African American image construction in the same positive way. In contrast, Black young boys are initially viewed as, less intelligent, troublemakers, aggressive, and lack cognitive aptitude. However, they are natural-born athletes and possibly criminals. As a result of this way of thinking, Black young boys are taught to be submissive, passive and quiet-spoken ... opposite traits of what a formidable, Transformational leader may possess. Add in the fact that these young, African American boys rarely witness positive male role models that look like them on a constant basis; you can understand how the problem of nullification by omission replicates and duplicates itself. The prototypes that are illuminated and fed to the world associated with African Americans by the System are images of slavery, athletes, entertainers, and criminals. These limited images confine African Americans to the margins ... never threatening the image of what a 'true-blooded' American is or what true intelligence looks like. Oprah and the others are viewed as just rare exceptions, anomalies.

The pressure to belong affects other groups as well as African Americans. As I have stated before, *everyone* is affected by the System, so the pressures of micro-aggression are transient. If a group rejects a set of prototypes, the willingness to assimilate and emulate the White construct, the 'dominant' power structure, emerges. For example, this is witnessed when individuals from ethnic groups change their names to American 'white' names such as John, or William, or Susie, or when they un-slant their eyes, bleach their skin, or straighten their hair. So, no one is untouched by the pressures of the System. Although it is extremely rare for a White American to undergo a procedure to slant their eyes or take an outside ethnic name like Cheng or Laquisha, as I mentioned earlier, some darken their skin, puff up their lips and so forth to modify their European design. However, they still remain within the construct of White, which carries a form of power. The distinction is located within the parameters of this power. This distinction calls for an analysis, then, of how power is distributed, how it is defined, how it is used, who gets to use it and where it is located.

Active Centralized Empowerment takes issue with all of these important elements and offers a form of navigation through meta-cognitive and critical thinking and a major propulsion of power.

CHAPTER 6
The Solution: Active Centralized Empowerment

African Americans must stop repeating behavior that simply does not work for us. The groundbreaking, action directed paradigm called Active Centralized Empowerment will lead to important debates and long-standing solutions that will change Black America in ways in which not only we live, but how we view ourselves and how Others view us as well. It is the first of its kind, theoretically and practically speaking, that African Americans can use on a daily basis to assist in their movement towards final freedom and liberation of the Self. This paradigm is like no other because, in its design, it offers solutions on a metacognitive level that results in the freeing of the mind from slavery, and consequently, an individual's potential and upward growth on many levels including economic as well as political. It is a different way of thinking, a different way of being and a different way of moving through one's life towards the goals of success and freedom through self-empowerment. I believe this theory, found on the fringes of Postmodernism, truly *rethinks* the challenge and approach to understanding Black America and transforms and transgresses by arguing that one must find their Situated Self in the core of their existence surrounded by attributes that make up the margins of Cross Cultural Competence. It rethinks what it is to be Black, what it is to be African American, by rethinking oneself and one's social location of empowerment.

Much like Lorber's Standpoint Theory, Active Centralized Empowerment is a "paradigm for the production of knowledge and culture that is critical of conventional wisdom and consciously aware of social location" for marginalized groups (Lorber, 2005, p. 176). It is a phenomenological argument. Collins argues that, "the significance of a Black feminist epistemology may lie in its ability to enrich our understanding of how subordinate groups create knowledge that fosters both their empowerment and social justice" (Collins, 2000, p.269). I propose this same type of formulaic argument when discussing

African Americans and Active Centralized Empowerment.

Active Centralized Empowerment does not allow for the focus to be on the blaming of particular individuals or the empowerment of others on ones existence and self-value. Instead, it liberates and encourages an individual to keep their focus on their own existence and development of their own self-empowerment and allows the focus in relation to others to be a construct of existence that can work together without negating each other or oppressing each other. In other words, I propose that A.C.E provides a working forum and safe environment where groups learn to work together through a process more like synergy rather than a hierarchical paradigm of power structure like what we see and operate within, today. As a researcher and social scientist, I further assert that Active Centralized Empowerment is a viable and important answer to the plight of not only the African American but, for any group or individual who feels marginalized in this country[21].

We know of the racist problems folded into the American fabric of this great nation but Active Centralized Empowerment (A.C.E.) is not about another race. It is not about only a System or an Institution. It is about knowing how to navigate your position *in relation* to the System and Institution. It is about knowing who YOU are in this WORLD, not simply this country, because you are bigger than this country and your purpose is BIGGER than this country. It is about knowing your Self and it begins and ends with YOUR BELIEF and the ACTIVATION of PERFORMING within that Belief. You are what you believe … so changing your belief, will change your life. We're going to do this by Re-defining Blackness … and getting you centralized. You will no longer be in the margins of someone else's Empire. You are an Empire with Self Agency, living and working within an eco-system comprised of your own merits, traits, characteristics, strengths, weaknesses, and goals.

To be centralized is to participate, be included, powerful, privileged, having a voice, connected, resourceful, positive self-economic positioning, influential, recognized and affirmed. Active Centralized Empowerment, argues that because of Cross Cultural Competence, instead of locating the individual on the margins of a group or System that they do not centrally belong to, an individual (I) can move from the margins to the center of their Situated Self, their own existence and core, and develop a sense of Self Agency (SA) comprised of the various characteristics that make them unique (Diagram 4).

Diagram 4. Marginalization to Active Centralized Empowerment

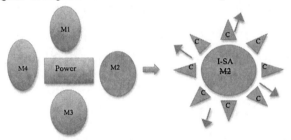

Diagram 4 illustrates the basic premise of A.C.E. movement. At the beginning the social location of the core controls the process and System - confining and limiting the ability of the Marginalized to navigate one's own existence to a place of empowerment. A.C.E. dictates that the Marginalized (M2)

individual remove and detach itself from this oppressive structure and locate this new Self Agency with power within the centralized location of your Situated Self.

This is done by taking those same elements of Marginalization that are used for oppressive reasons and transforming them into elements of empowerment based on Cross Cultural Competence. In other words, speaking and moving from experience and Situated Knowledge that is separate but equal and empowered. They are now centralized. Barbara Smith describes this difference, writing, "autonomy and separatism are fundamentally different, whereas autonomy comes from a position of strength, separatism comes from a position of fear" (Collins, P. 37, 2000) and "when we're truly autonomous we can deal with other kinds of people, a multiplicity of issues, and with difference, because we have formed a solid base of strength" (Smith, xl, 1983). Separatism, which is what we have in today's system of human navigation, is the position of fear and resistance that dictates outward and internalized marginalization and always operates from a position dictated by a core of power outside of oneself. Centralized autonomy, on the other hand, is powerful. This solid base of Strength with Autonomy is YOU, your Self Agency, during Active Centralized Empowerment, located away from the margins of an Oppressive System. In Hartsock's essay (2004), Political Change: Two Perspectives on Power, she explains power as "creative, life-affirming, definition (definitives) that equate power with the ability to act with strength and ability, or with action that brings a sense of accomplishment ... and effective interaction (p. 91)." So, by being in control of who we are and how we navigate through our lives outside of a construct that is not designed for our own happiness, allows us to move freely between the two worlds. We have the power, in other words.

Diagram 5 further illustrates how A.C.E. centralizes a person through a conversion process using attributes typically/stereotypically assigned to a marginalized, young, African American male or female who is subjectively viewed. These negative ID labels with negative connotations such as Minority, Loose, Nigger and "Babies Mamas" are usually used to justify a form of oppression.

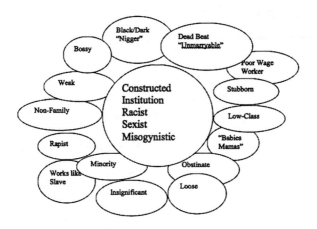

Diagram 5. Attributes *Perceived* from a Racist, Misogynistic, Sexist Institution

Contrary to Cooley's Looking Glass Self as I proposed earlier, in A.C.E., the marginalized individual disconnects from the oppressive construct by first, redefining and reconstructing these same labels into labels that are more accurate, appropriate and carry value originating from a different belief system. A belief system that says although others may marginalize me, I know there is power, knowledge and value in my experiences

131

(Standpoint Theory and Situated, Socialized Self) so I am going to redefine my Self as such. So instead of viewing herself or himself as a dead beat, not worth marrying, mother or father, who is poor and lazy … the individual now views him or herself as a single parent who is self-sufficient who knows how to work on a budget.

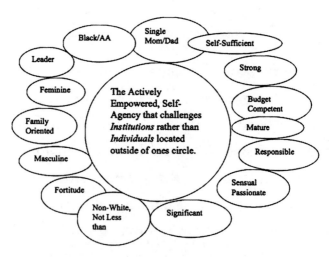

Diagram 6. Redefined Attributes

This form of centralized empowerment

encourages the individual to redefine themselves without blaming others or a system or giving others or a system power over who they are. It is widely known and accepted that, in some instances, African Americans have to work twice, even three times harder than the non-black worker for less credit, reward, and validation in the traditional module that is used today in this capitalistic society[22]. The traditional, customary re-dress of the marginalized would consist of them simply working harder in hopes that the oppressor will change in time. Instead of feeling sorry for yourself as a victim or Marginalized victim, A.C.E. encourages the individual to accept this knowledge as a shortcoming of the System or the oppressor and then begin to work differently and smarter. The individual practicing A.C.E. will then feel self-empowered to ask for a raise, a more appropriate title, or some form of positive acknowledgment of their work and value or even a change in location.

Another example of A.C.E. in movement would be instead of seeing yourself as a single mom of three, located on the bottom rung of society who works every day (can't afford to miss a day), makes lunch, balances and pays the bills, and resolves conflicts between siblings … you redefine the value of your work and redefine what others deem as negative into a proactive positive. Now, through A.C.E., you view yourself as an effective mediator and negotiator with effective communication skills because of your single mom status. You can also add dependable, independent, trustworthy and responsible. These examples reveal how A.C.E. allows the marginalized individual to find and define their place in the world and begin moving from that location that is deemed appropriate, accurate and fair. It's how they see themselves, their own knowledge and understanding through their experiences that matter. These redefined positive attributes not only moves the individual away from the margins of oppression as they navigate their lives, the margins are now strong conduits they can use to help navigate their lives with other people and other institutions. In other words, their Identity and Sense of Self is not predicated on the belief systems of others, therefore, synergy is encouraged. Furthermore, this location of proactive empowerment also encourages others to view this person in a different light (Diagram 7).

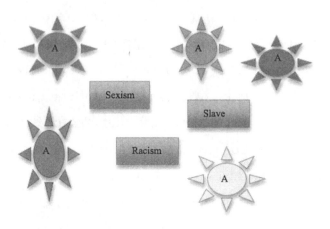

Diagram 7. ACE in Movement

Additionally, there is accountability on both sides that requires each individual to live up to the redefined labels and adjust their lives accordingly. The existentialist argument is that this way of navigating allows each individual ecosystem that is built from specific characteristics and beliefs as well as goals, to be relocated in the margins of <u>their own existence</u>. Therefore, allowing self-agency and free movement to be activated. Therefore, not only is the movement of A.C.E. not oppressive to the individual, this movement is not oppressive to others. The subject does not necessarily collide or fall victim to the power structures of others. They merely move from one structure to another through self-empowerment and Cross Cultural Competence (Situated Knowledge) but never completely joining outside structures. This allows for the protection of self-identity and de-marginalization of oppressive measures. Simultaneously, this process develops and enhances all parties' sense of self-knowing and self-value. I further propose that this model allows for movement of an individual that is more closely related to their Authentic Self- an important process in the development of Agency and improved Self-Esteem (feeling good internally)[23]. In similar fashion, the African American Male, specifically, navigates his existence in a manner that allows self-defined masculinity and performance. The African side of the Black Male (as well as Female) is extremely important in this instance because it automatically makes the subject Global and more than just a descendant of slaves. He/she is both. So, instead of fighting their way back from a negative sense of Self prescribed to them such as "boy," "nigger," lazy, criminal, and so forth, through A.C.E. and a re-education of who he is as an African American Male, the Black Males can form a sense of Self Agency comprised of being African, African American, Spiritual, originated from Kings-Chiefs, warriors, natural leaders, powerful, inner and outer strength, courageous, resilient, and masculine. It is from these labels of Self that he will perform (Image 1).

Image 1. Black American Male Empowered
as African American Male

What this also means is that when he is called out of his name or treated less than, he will view this form of micro-aggression as a problem of the messenger, not himself. Therefore, he is no longer a slave to the perceptions and intended performances dictated by oppressors as well. He simply navigates within his existence through developing his own world and sense of Self without losing his own identity or being subjected to identities others place upon him if he doesn't want to. In this egalitarian type of environment that dictates respect for differences, the Black Male can go to work but not become his work, work with other males, genders and races but not become a part of their ecosystem and vice versa. He understands the limited knowledge and experience that prohibit others to judge him fairly at times and is able to view this as their problem and not his. This disconnection from validation from others enables him to navigate as a man, Black Man and African American Man, freely. He can navigate his life as an American as a Self Agent within his own ecosystem without being oppressed by others ... and vice versa. Knowing and embracing their Authentic Selves, Black males will engage in actions and performances of mature responsibility and leadership and serve as protectors, and providers, just to name a few.

African American women can do the same. Black women are being called out of their names and sexually objectified with no one defending them, out loud! The moment that they embrace the fact that they come from a line of royalty, queens, leaders, matriarchs of humanity, hard workers, versatile in child rearing, etc. they will find honor and pride and begin or continue to move in a positive direction. This part of the process is absolutely necessary for the survival of the African American woman because they do not have any messages of these positive attributes as a part of their lives on a daily basis. Besides the individual being impacted, without this positive way of viewing themselves and performing within this position of power, they are limited in terms of the kinds of parents they can become. African American women will continue to be limited in not only the capacity to nurture their children, for example, but also their ability to pass on this legacy, as a people. This awareness is also imperative because the women are the matriarchs of the Black, African American family! Without their *healthy* leadership and nurturing ways, the black family will continue to suffer. They will not be able to provide a solid foundation for their children nor the self-confidence that comes from knowing who you are from childhood. From childhood, Pam W.[24], an African American that I interviewed for this book, said that her immediate family as well as her extended family were all dysfunctional. There was limited, if any, nurturing or support within her family. "I believe, both, my mother and father were dysfunctional because *their* mothers and fathers were much the same. They didn't know any better," she said. It is a set of skills that were absent from generation to generation. Pam found hope during a 2-month stay with an African family in Illinois. She enjoyed her visit, thoroughly, and said that the thing that had the most impact on her life was the sense of family - a different kind of family than she was used to. "I saw that *family* was truly first. Everyone played a role and every role was to support and nurture anyone who needed it, from whatever family they came from," she said. So, family did not necessarily mean, blood-related. It meant being there for one another as a *collective* and being there in a nurturing and positive way. As an African American, this was not her experience in her immediate family, and unfortunately, it is not the experience of many other African Americans.

By developing your own ecosystem through A.C.E., a person is no longer strictly confined to proving or disproving someone else's judgment and prejudices of them (Image 2).

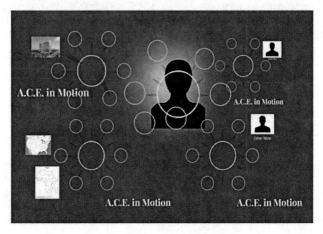

Image 2. A.C.E. in Motion

One can acknowledge their views without fighting for power. More like 'agree to disagree' scenario that can be very helpful at times.

The basic understanding for the A.C.E. individual is that an individual can live, work, and operate within an informal or formal construct without necessarily playing an engaging and supportive role in a racist, discriminatory, sexist or oppressive agenda. Because A.C.E. dictates that in some instances, the blame should not be on the individuals themselves who do not and did not design the System that perpetuates this racist ideology, I propose that there can be some effectiveness through the engagement of A.C.E. for White Americans/European Americans. We do this by examining particular areas, such as areas of diversity, or lack thereof, within companies, corporations, classrooms, newsrooms, etc. and the demographics of persons in leadership positions. An example of this type of movement would be when a White American decides to disconnect from the racist infrastructure and reveals ways his/her company practices racial discrimination.

They can file an official report, choose not to participate in such acts, inform the oppressive group members that they will not condone or be a part of a racist agenda, or inform the target of the discrimination. Or when a heterosexual person decides not to partake in acts of homophobia by joining an Ally group. Or they choose to turn away from acts of buying into a counterproductive structure when, while they share some of the same beliefs as some people involved in hate crimes, they acknowledge that the act of killing and violence is wrong so they don't participate. In other words, Active Centralized Empowerment allows an individual to be who they are at the moment and choose a specific direction that will lead to balance and fairness, which is closer to a 'changed' belief system as well as their authentic Self.

Finally, by allowing each member to dictate their own worth and value, strengthens the group/culture/nation (America) as a whole and respects the space and boundaries of others. An example of this part of the process occurs when a White American, engaging in A.C.E., decides to hoist the confederate flag in *their own* backyard versus a *main interstate* that represents and speaks for an entire state. Although the Civil War was fought and the Union won and we say the pledge of allegiance to one flag, as one nation, under God, there are some who still believe they should have the right to wave the confederate flag anywhere and everywhere in this country. Active Centralized Empowerment encourages them to exhibit their southern pride[25] in the privacy of their sphere (respecting freedom of expression and speech), without disrespecting others. Strangely enough, however, this type of thinking is not the case in many states. I use the word "strangely" because I have witnessed White Americans who are not from the south actually adopt the confederacy arguments and standpoints as if they were. Additionally, I find it a bit "strange" that, time and time again, the debates over the confederacy and the "south will rise again" motto rarely involve northern White Americans. Why is it that African Americans are usually the ones taking up the mantle of justice to say what is and isn't offensive? Shouldn't White Northerners have something to say about it? I propose that this is an example of how White Pride and Southern Pride are one in the same in many ways. More importantly, this example also exemplifies the ubiquitous nature of the racist structure/System operationalized in America I have spoken about, one that minimizes the worth of a group in place of individual freedoms.

Despite and in spite of the racist, oppressive structures we live and work in, non-Blacks and non-African Americans, individuals from the dominant core structure of power, regardless of "birth right," choose not to follow the crowd of racism each and every day. A.C.E. gives them the opportunity to make their own decisions and be judged based upon their own actions instead of being prejudged, based upon their race or color of their skin, or even belief. Translated, a White American should not be assumed to be racist and discriminatory just because they are White. An African American male should not be prejudged as a criminal because they are Black. This gives everyone a fair opportunity to grow and move freely. If it is determined that a White person is racist and discriminatory, they can still be judged fairly and freely because that is just who they are. With this truth, individuals can decide to change, or not, and outside individuals can decide to stay connected with them, or not. This process can be engaged in the classroom, the work place, home, or in society in general. Furthermore, by examining the System instead of the individual, directly, will allow individuals who may have been brought up a certain way, to safely voice their beliefs so that there is a better understanding by all. This means, Black and White Americans, together, will work to change/dismantle the System, instead of feeling personally attacked. Remember that the goal of A.C.E. is not to place individual agendas on the backs of others, but to challenge the System, the root of the problem that upholds individual and collective injustices through self-agency and self-empowerment. In the meantime, by merely having an understanding and a respect between two diverse cultures should be viewed as a big and important change that should not be dismissed.

6.2:
Lifting the Veil

Much like lifting the veil from someone's eyes, African Americans using the process of A.C.E. will see clearer and view situations and happenings in a new way. This also means that they will navigate their lives differently as well. The African American who uses A.C.E. will view being descendants of slavery as a position of honor, strength, bravery and courage derived and passed on to them from the strong Africans who were able to survive the Middle Passage and all of its atrocities. That, despite all of the discriminatory, racist, sexist exploits that continue today, African Americans are still standing. Through the visualization and engagement in A.C.E., AAs will realize that because there were no formal reparations, African Americans are crippled, financially, now and for generations to come. They will realize that by investing in each other as other aggregates have the damage can be slowed. This would also include members of other races investing in your healing as well. Instead of working from the position of victim, through the prism of A.C.E., the African American will realize that we make up one of the largest groups of consumers and by simply boycotting products or companies who treat us unfairly, can be extremely effective. There will be a realization that each time we call each other out of our names with such words as "Nigger," WE are giving others permission to engage in forms of entitlement that says that they can do the same. We will realize that Black tokenism still exists when our Black voices are not respected or included as a voice of expertise and authority on issues of Blackness and racial injustice, not to mention other areas of expertise that are not race-focused. We will realize that it is wrong to financially support Time Share Resorts built on plantations that were built from the blood, sweat and sufferings of our African ancestors. We will realize every time we seek validation from the oppressor of the System, we are empowering them and in cases when validation is given, sometimes it merely means that the result is something they can accept, not necessarily the truth and what is best for you. The Active Centralized Empowered African American realizes that Black on Black crime has to stop and gang members need to have a voice but not always possess the only platform for Black America. Through Active Centralized Empowerment, instead of killing communities and individuals with guns and drugs, gang members who have been left behind and out of the "American Dream," will see that they have a bigger purpose, their lives have a bigger purpose. They will turn and use their minds, some of them brilliant, for services that uplift the community, build a community, as they thrive in the community. We will realize that when we engage in shameless displays of self-hate and hate of one another, we are only hurting ourselves and our momentum to move forward and upwards, as a people. We will realize that to solve a lot of our problems means getting to the root of the problem. This includes having compassion for African Americans who are allowing their own hurt and pain to be exploited in the Media just to make money. We will realize that we shouldn't support those who do not support us. We will realize that within our culture and blood, we have particular mores, traditions, rituals and beliefs. We will realize that we raise our children differently. Like Africans, we spank them when needed, we don't allow them to call us by our first name, drink coffee or liquor with us, or smoke cigarettes in front of us at an early age and we have the belief system that states sometimes, children are to be seen and not heard, especially when it comes to adult conversation. We will realize, as educators, that when we have asked students to call us by our titles, and they refuse to do so, and their parents allow their children to also ignore this request, you, your place of respect, authority, as well as your culture are being dismissed.

Through Active Centralized Empowerment, when the metacognitive process of severing the "umbilical cord of slavery" connected to beliefs of less than, minority, weaker than, is engaged and completed, the pain and suffering found when others propel their racist insults or other offenses onto your being is minimized. It is now, You, who determines the level of effect and depth of such insults and acts as well as the power of such judgment may have over you. You now decide whether to let any of this into your sphere of existence. Because YOU make this decision, unlike the *Looking Glass Self* and some processes of Marginalization that teaches to fight only from the margins, you have the ability to move freely and proactively in the creation of your space, place of happiness, peace and empowerment[26]. This also means that because YOU make the decision, based upon your active belief system, you must live up to the positive images put forth. Failing to do this means the failure of not only the individual, but also, possibly, the African American culture and race as a collective. And while you're navigating through the American side of your Blackness ... the African side of yourself will truly set you free as well.

Historically and ancestrally-speaking, if you are Black and if you are African American, you are probably descendants of a group of people who were strong enough to survive the Middle Passage and strong enough to build MANY countries, including America. You helped build and operate the pyramids, the first schools, agricultural methods that fed nations, designed the first religions and places of worship, language, science, philosophy, math, literature and you were some of the FIRST LEADERS, Kings and Queens, for all others to follow. So the paradigm of A.C.E. movement for the Ancestrally-centered African American, including the attribute of Cross Cultural Competence (CCC), extends and completes the individual even further and deeper (Diagram 8).

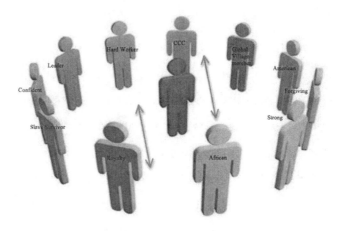

Diagram 8. Ancestral Movement of A.C.E. AFRICAN American

Active Centralized Empowerment offers a new way of moving through life, a new way of thinking about your position, your value and your power and self worth for anyone who wants to be involved. In an ideal world, within the engaging environment of Active Centralized Empowerment, individuals with various trades, traits, characteristics, gender, sex, race, ethnicity and nationalities gain momentum and Freely spin its structure of self agency from one round culture to another yet never losing its true identity and power. Never colliding with one another or oppressing and negating one another. Simply, moving close to one another as their authentic selves, working toward a common goal, without melting into each other, or losing ones own identity in exchange for another (Diagram 9).

Diagram 9. Active Centralized Empowerment
engagement by the Masses

Let what I am going to say next, serve as both a warning and as a position of empowerment through Knowledge. One CANNOT do ANY of these things without Self Awareness, Self-Concept or Self-Efficacy. To engage in Active Centralized Empowerment using the Authentic Self *demands* for you to be AWARE of who you are in spite or despite outside influence from others. This is where existentialist knowledge of who you are from your experience as well as who you are historically and culturally derives. From this point, you gain an active, constructed as well as a constructive CONCEPT of who you are, as a developing Self in action. In other words, you perform within the definition and concept of who you know yourself to be. Your TRUE Self. The definition of Self Efficacy "refers to an individual's belief in his or her capacity to execute behaviors necessary to produce specific performance attainments (Bandura, 1977, 1986, 1997)." It is the "confidence in the ability to exert control over one's own motivation, behavior, and social environment."[27] So, the next time a person who *is not* African American or Black American tells you that there is no Black Experience or Culture, you will not immediately feel marginalized, retreating to a place of disempowerment called the Spiral of Silence, and say nothing. You have a voice that represents YOUR TRUTH and should be acknowledged as such. Even if your truth is

NOT acknowledged, the practice and process in engaging in the narratives that define you is life changing and empowering!

If followed, A.C.E. can truly serve as a way of being free and performing within that freedom to be who you are; the POSITIVE and EMPOWERING person you were MEANT TO BE! You will pull your pants up, take off your hats at the appropriate times, watch your language, believe in yourself, therefore, performing better, respect women, protect the ones who need protection, gain self-respect and self-appreciation and engage in actions that bring you, your people, your country and all of its inhabitants and your ancestral country, PRIDE.

CHAPTER 7

Conclusion

I have argued that African Americans must stop repeating behavior that simply does not work for us. At this point and time, although other countries and their fellow men and women have received formal apologies and reparations, African Americans, by and large, have not. Because America as a country exists as a result of the exploitation of free labor demanded of the Africans as slaves, I believe there should be some form of reparations. Preferably land, free college education or discounted rate, 2 DNA tests per family from AfricanAncestry.com[28], and free access to reputable genealogy databases, so that our destroyed lineage can be reconnected. Lacking these major tools of navigation has crippled the African American people and America, as a country. Because we did not receive land, we had/have no geographical or generational wealth or economic wealth that has longevity. A quality education was denied us decades ago, and when given, sub-par education was the choice, which hurt our job prospects from that point on as an aggregate. And to be denied a legacy and history beyond the borders of the United States has harmed us interpersonally as well as intra-personally, placing us in a never ending position of "minority" and Marginalization. I would argue that upon receiving these tools, used for survival and prosperity by other aggregates, African Americans could finally begin living the American Dream on equal footing, geographically as well as economically, and as a Collective Identity. But, to acknowledge this assertion will take some time because there are others who must go through a healing process as well.

I have also explained how the processes of Marginalization, Symbolic Interactionism and Cooley's Looking Glass Self work harmoniously to keep African Americans oppressed and disempowered within a System that was founded and built on racism. African Americans must come to an understanding that the present day System was not designed for them to succeed. Because they have operated within this System from the margins, they have become supporters of this racist System, unknowingly, and have developed Internalized Colonization and

Racial Fatigue. This conditioning can be overcome. It is time for African Americans to take the important step that no one else will take and simply extend forgiveness so that we can move on, so that we can get to work on improving our lives and so that NO ONE easily disempowers us, prohibiting our ability to navigate our lives. It is time to break the chains of enslavement. It's time for African Americans to recapture what was stolen from them, their roots located in the spiritual ground that they walk on here in America and abroad. It is time that we re-construct our images and our sense of Self that speaks to our Authentic Selves … our Factual Selves. It is time for US to re-educate ourselves and tell our stories about our experiences and about our solutions. It is time to redefine our Blackness, break the chains of oppression that are placed on us by others and by ourselves, by being Transformational leaders who say that we will no longer use the N-word or any other derogatory labels in public. We will hold our other brothers and sisters accountable for the same and not involve ourselves in Black hate and Self-hate. It is time that African Americans adopt a paradigm that is tailored to address our challenges ... instead of consistently trying to emulate and assimilate into a Systemic culture that continues to disempower who we are. It is time to engage in Active Centralized Empowerment.

I assert that this groundbreaking, game-changing paradigm and module has the potential to change all of America, not just Black America. Active Centralized Empowerment provides a basic and fundamental foundation to understanding all of the other debates, calls for action and movement in present day conversations and discourses on race. It will change how we view ourselves, consequently, how Others view and interact with us as well. This paradigm is unique because it dictates movement to the core of power as its central focus by the individuals and aggregates found in the margins. It is the first of its kind, theoretically and practically speaking, that African Americans can use on a daily basis to assist in their movement towards final freedom and liberation of the Self. A.C.E. offers solutions on a metacognitive level that frees the mind from slavery, and consequently, an individual's potential and upward growth on many levels including economic as well as political. It is a different way of thinking, a different way of being and a different way of moving through one's life towards the goals of success and freedom through self-empowerment.

Active Centralized Empowerment does not allow for the focus to be on the blaming of particular individuals or the empowerment of others on ones existence and self-value. Instead, it liberates and encourages an individual to keep their focus on their own existence and development of their own self-empowerment and allows the focus, in relation to others, to be a construct of existence that can work together without negating each other or oppressing each other. Active Centralized Empowerment asks that you take responsibility to <u>know better</u> and <u>do better</u>. To not allow yourself to simply be defined by others so that THEIR world works better. You must redefine YOURSELF with empowering truthful facts so that YOU can work better in YOUR world that is a part of the WHOLE world. Active Centralized Empowerment says to pull yourself up from within. Within your minds and the captivity of your souls and embrace the fact that you are important and worthy and you have played important roles in developing not only this country, but also, the world. You can no longer wait for others to change. You must change your thinking, your minds and your beliefs. This will allow you to move to a place of empowerment rather than remain in the margins of oppression. Then, Black Americans, African Americans, including Black men, can finally become the leaders they were always meant to be. It is time for the rejuvenation, redesign and rebirth of the Black American, the African American image so that they can be judged fairly and treated fairly. You are no longer slaves. YOU are no longer a slave so you must be and become and perform as the Free American and the African American you were born to be.

What I have written in some portions of this book is about a BLACK EXPERIENCE. Individuals outside of this Blackness will not *fully understand*, even if they tried, and wanted to, because they are not Black. However, it is important that they understand this process and how they can support or hinder the efforts of equality that it affords. Like most great movements and success, no one group from the margins can do it alone. It takes a rainbow of individuals to make the world a better place ... but your healing must begin with you. The message is only as strong as the receiver so the sooner you begin to re-educate yourselves, others, and the world ... the better. I encourage you to engage in Active Centralized Empowerment ... and view yourself, your struggles and your opportunities in a different light. Stop seeing yourselves as slaves. Stop acting like slaves and know that you are powerful within the roots inside of you. Know that with this knowledge, you can do anything you put your mind to … which is simply learning to navigate through your life empowered. Through Active Centralized Empowerment you should know that you can be whoever you want to be, achieve whatever you want to achieve, even love whomever you want to love. And the Leaders that emerge from this positive place of love, self love and the love for others to do the same will truly guide people and cultures and societies to a higher understanding and place of fulfillment and contentment that is truly empowering. There is value and power in perspectives and experiences that originate from multiplicities of Self. I submit that everyone, of every race and ethnicity should engage in Active Centralized Empowerment and work to break down the racist System that has so many of us enslaved in this country. As Black and Whites and other races and ethnicities work, together, for the common good, the old, racist and oppressive System will weaken - eventually ceasing to exist, slowly dismantling itself. I believe that by successfully dismantling this System, we can begin to build a strong and peaceful world where ALL people can flourish. The beautiful type of freedom that I see illuminate, brightly, from the eyes of African Americans when I tell them that surviving slavery is only the tip of the iceberg of their strength and who they really are. It's the joy and the sigh of relief that fills the room when I see my White American students and friends dance with "soul" rather than "control," smile because mistakes are acceptable and they don't have to be perfect, or smile because they do not have to lead the charge for *everything* and *everybody*.[29] They relieve themselves of White guilt by simply being free without racial dictation. It is the best result of Active Centralized Empowerment.

So the next time you find yourself in a racist/sexist/oppressive situation, ask yourself, did you ACE it? Did you move yourself from the margins and stand firm in your own core of empowerment, and elevate yourself to a better understanding? I wish this for you … my sisters and brothers, of every race, gender, sex, creed, ethnicity and sexual orientation. I wish this for you. Together, it can be done.

References

Berger, Peter. *Invitation to Sociology: A Humanistic Perspective*. New York: Doubleday. 1963.

Berger, Peter. and Luckman, Thomas. *The Social Constructs of Reality*. New York: Doubleday. 1967.

Blumer, Herbert. *Symbolic Interactionism: Perspective and Method*. New Jersey: Prentice-Hall. 1969.

Bradley, Harriet. *Fractured Identities: Changing Patterns of Inequality*. Polity and Blackwell: Cambridge. 1996.

Charon, Joel. *Symbolic Interactionism: An Introduction, An Interpretation, An Integration*. New Jersey: Pearson Education. 2004.

Collins, Janice Marie. <u>Distorted Snapshots of Reality: Role Representation and Image Portrayals of African American, White American,</u>

Hispanic and Asian American Characters in Prime-time Television Commercials. Thesis. Ohio University, 2005. http://books.google.com/books/about/Distorted_Snapshots_of_Reality.html?id=C6dPNwAACAAJ

Collins, Janice Marie. Finding Leadership in the "Real World" of News: The Professional Socialization of Leadership Development and Issues of Power, Gender, Race, and Self Esteem in a College Broadcast Journalism Lab, A Case Study. Diss. Ohio University, 2009. https://etd.ohiolink.edu/rws_etd/document/get/ohiou1236724544/inline

Collins, Patricia Hill. "Learning from the Outsider Within: The Sociological Significance of Black Feminist Thought." Pp. 103-126 in *The Feminist standpoint Theory Reader: Intellectual & Political Controversies* edited by Sandra Harding. New York: Routledge. 2004.

Collins, Patricia Hill. *Gender, Black Feminism and Black Political Economy. The Annals of the American Academy of Political and Social Science*, March, 41-53, 2000.

Collins, Patricia Hill. *Black Feminist Thought: Knowledge, Consciousness, and the Politics of Empowerment. 10th edition.* New York: Routledge. 2000.

References

Collins, Patricia Hill. *It's all in the Family: Intersections of Gender, Race, and Nation. Hypatia*, Summer,13 (3), 62-83. 1998.

Cooley, Charles Horton. *Human Nature and the Social Order*, Scribner's, NY, pp.179-185. 1902.

Entman, Robert, Rojecki, Andrew. *The Black Image in the White Mind: Media and Race in America.* Chicago and London, University of Chicago Press. 2000.

Gramscii, Antonio. Cultural Themes: Ideological Material. In Meenakshi Gigi Durham & Douglas M. Kellner, (Eds.), *Media and Cultural Studies: Keyworks* (pp.43-47). Malden, MA: Blackwell Publishing. 2001.

Hall, Stuart and Hobson Dorothy, Love Andrew, Willis Paul. "Encoding/decoding." *Culture, Media, Language: Working Papers in Cultural Studies*, 1972-1979. London: Hutchinson. 1980.

Harding, Sandra. *The Feminist Standpoint Theory Reader.* New York: Routledge Publishing. 2004.

Hartsock, Nancy. *The Feminist Standpoint: Developing the Ground for A Specifically Feminist Historical Materialism. In Sandra Harding, (Ed.), The Feminist Standpoint Theory Reader: Intellectual & Political Controversies* (pp. 35-54). New York: Routledge. 2004.

179

Heider, Don. *White News: Why Local News Programs Don't Cover People of Color*. Mahwah, NJ: Lawrence Erlbaum Associates. 2000.

Holstein, James A., and Gubrium, Jaber F. *The Self We Live By: Narrative Identity in a Postmodern World*. NY: Oxford University Press. 2000.

hooks, bell. "Choosing the Margin as a Space of Radical Openness." Pp. 153-160 in *The Feminist standpoint Theory Reader: Intellectual & Political Controversies* edited by Sandra Harding. New York: Routledge. 2004.

hooks, bell. *Feminist Theory: From Margin to Center*. Boston, MA: South End Press. 1984.

hooks, bell. *Teaching to Transgress: Education as the Practice of Freedom*. NY: Routledge. 1994.

Jensen, Robert. *The Heart of Whiteness: Confronting Race, Racism, and White Privilege*. San Francisco, CA. City Lights Bookstore. 2000.

Lehrer, Keith. *Theory of Knowledge*. Boulder, CO. Westview Press. 2000

Leigh, Robert D., editor, *A Free and Responsible Press: A General Report on Mass Communication: Newspapers, Radio, Motion Pictures, Magazines, and Books by the Commission on Freedom of the Press*. Chicago: University of Chicago Press.1947.

References

Lorber, Judith. *Gender Inequality: Feminist Theories and Politics*. 3rd Edition. Oxford University Press. 2007.

Smith, Barbara. *Home Girls: A Black Feminist Anthology*. Rutgers University Press. 2000.

United States. *Kerner Commission. Report of the National Advisory Commission on Civil Disorders*. 1968. Washington: U.S. Government Printing Office.

Van Zoonen, Liesbet. *Feminist Media Studies*. Thousand Oaks, California: Sage Publications. 1994.

Williams, Vanessa. "On 'Finding your roots,' how you became you." *The Washington Post*, LexisNexis Pg. T03, (March 25, 2012), viewed 12/16/2012.

Yeung, King-To, and Martin, John Levi. "The Looking Glass Self: An Empirical Test and Elaboration." *Social Forces* 81, no. 3, 843-879. 2003: http://www.fbi.gov/about-us/cjis/ucr/hate-crime/2012/topic-pages/incidents-and-offenses/incidentsandoffenses_final. Tables 3, 42, 43. Visited April 12, 2014

Endnotes

1 People in general, are slaves within an oppressive System, this oppressive System that I am referring. So, regardless of race, ethnicity, gender, sex, sexual orientation, etc…individuals can relate to this System of oppression.

2 Not everyone looks good in natural styles so weaves, perms that don't strip your hair are quite alright… as long as these processes of transformation don't change "Who" you are…a person of color

3 "Colorism" is alive and well, even from other African American women…it must stop

4 I will not delve further into the many injustices of various groups at this time because I support Elizabeth Spellman's argument that it is not wise to compare sufferings between various marginalized groups; instead, allow each group to have its own voice and

experience. So, for this particular writing, I will focus on the plight of the African American.

5 For this reason, White represents the Construct of Whiteness that is developed and designed, and not simply a white person

6 An example of this would be for every white man who possesses these characteristics to be viewed as a racist without regard to the individual perspectives and feelings.

7 Zimmerman stated that he was not racist because he was a mentor to young black boys without incident

8 This article appeared in The Washington Post July 15, 2013…titled, Richard Cohen: Racism vs. Reality

9 Data taken from the 2012 FBI annual reports on crime, Tables 42 and 43

10 Data taken from the 2012 FBI Hate Crime Statistics, Table 3

11 Same Washington Post column written by Cohen on July 15, 2013 titled Richard Cohen: Racism vs. Reality

12 I can also include the fact that some Africans view African Americans much in the same manner

13 I also conducted similar studies that included

other aggregates including women and Hispanics of people of Latin descent.

14 A copy of my dissertation can be located in the references that analyzed leadership development by gender, race and issues of power and self-esteem

15 You can find one of my studies using this link https://etd.ohiolink.edu/rws_etd/document/get/ ohiou1236724544/inline

16 You can read my thesis study through Ohio University, Distorted Snapshots of Reality found in the Bibliography

17 The various reality programs with predominantly Black casts

18 These acts are no different than other groups and individuals who kill or hurt innocent victims as well because they are angry. The difference is that most of the time, people of color are portrayed as the perpetrators more prevalently.

19 Subsequent Genealogy focused programs reveal displays of emotions when Whtie Americans discover their roots OUTSIDE of America, which is different from the African American's responses.

20 I do not include Native Americans or Indigenous Americans in this argument. This aggregate is a full-study on its own and I feel it would be an injustice to

group them with this argument so simply and easily.

21 I am also writing short manuals on ACE for women, members of the LGBTQ culture, the classroom, and individuals-in general. I believe it was a form of ACE that elected President Obama for office, twice. Marginalized groups used their individual characteristics to develop power to move from the margins to the core, making a difference and major changes.

22 This is also the case for women

23 I have used a form of ACE in my classes over the past 4 years and not only is there an increase in performance representation of self-confidence, and Transformational Leadership, there is also an increase in the students self-esteem scores

24 I am only using the first letter of her last name to protect her privacy.

25 Some "northerners" also partake in this activity

26 An example of this type of ACE movement that involves a number of Marginalized aggregates that found their empowerment is the election, twice, of President Obama. Groups that were marginalized and discounted, young, various races and ethnicities (white, black, Hispanic, etc), lgbtqa community members, moved in the same direction with the same goal. Collectively, they are stronger and bigger.

27 Definition taken from the American Psychological Association website on January 24, 2015 at https://www.google.com/search?client=safari&rls=en&q=self+efficacy&ie=UTF-8&oe=UTF-8

28 I encourage you to use the DNA testing found at Africanancestry.com to do this. Read it carefully to find out which person should take the test for the optimum results.

29 Correlation between races and suicides should be studies

If you would like to invite Dr. Janice Collins to your events as a guest speaker or would like to request her services as a Life Coach or Media Specialist please email her at Aceactivated@outlook.com

CPSIA information can be obtained
at www.ICGtesting.com
Printed in the USA
FFOW01n1914110615
14140FF